Standing the Gaff

"STEAMBOAT" JOHNSON
Standing the Gaff for 25 years

STANDING THE GAFF

The Life and Hard Times of a Minor League Umpire

By "Steamboat" Johnson

Introduction to the Bison Book Edition by Larry R. Gerlach

University of Nebraska Press
Lincoln and London

Manufactured in the United States of America

First Bison Book printing: 1994
Most recent printing indicated by the last digit below:
10 9 8 7 6 5 4 3 2 1

Library of Congress Cataloging-in-Publication Data
Johnson, Harry, 1884–1951.
Standing the gaff: the life and hard times of a minor league umpire / by "Steamboat" Johnson; introduction to the Bison Book edition by Larry R. Gerlach.
p. cm.
Originally published: Nashville, Tenn.: Parthenon Press, © 1935. With new introd.
"Bison."
Includes index.
Includes bibliographical references.
ISBN 0-8032-7579-X
1. Johnson, Harry, 1884–1951. 2. Baseball umpires—United States—Biography. 3. Minor leagues—United States—History. I. Title.
GV865.J597 1994
796.357'3'092—dc20
[B]
93-30952 CIP

Originally printed for "Steamboat Johnson" by the Parthenon Press, Nashville, Tenn., in 1935. A subtitle has been added to this Bison Book edition.

∞

Contents

Illustrations

Introduction

by Larry R. Gerlach

"I'm Harry Johnson, new Southern umpire." With that bald introduction, the stranger with a booming voice handed Herbert Caldwell, sports editor of the Memphis *Commercial Appeal*, a clipping from a small weekly paper in Michigan. Superimposed above a brief story about the afternoon's game and extending over the entire width of the page was the headline: "HARRY JOHNSON WILL UMPIRE TODAY." "That's me," grinned the newly arrived Yankee.[1] It was April 1919: Johnson's umpirial conquest of Dixie had begun.

One of the most popular arbiters who ever bellowed a strike or ducked a bottle, "Steamboat" Johnson belied the notion that baseball fans don't pay to see the umpires. He also rejected the old adage that an arbiter had done a good job if after the game fans did not remember who umpired. Knowing well that tough calls against the home team were always unpopular, he averred: "When fans squawk you can tell the umpire is doing the job right, but woe unto the umpire when the crowd is silent."[2]

Beloved by fans and players alike, he was a good umpire and a great gate attraction. Sportswriters and fans invariably described him in the most vivid terms. More than forty years after Steamboat's death, veteran Memphis sportswriter George Lapidis remembered him: "He was the most colorful umpire I've ever seen, and I've seen [Bill] Klem and all of them."[3]

Were there a Minor League Baseball Hall of Fame, Steamboat Johnson would be the first umpire inducted. Except for fifty-four games as a National League umpire in 1914, he spent his career callin' 'em in the "bush leagues." He worked more seasons and more games in the minor leagues than any other umpire in history.[4] During thirty-seven consecutive seasons (1910–1946), he umpired more than 5,700 games. (The only professional umpires to work more seasons—and therefore probably more games—than Johnson are major leaguers Bill Klem, forty; Bob Emslie, thirty-nine; and Tommy Connolly and Bill McGowan, thirty-eight each.) An "iron man in blue," Johnson reportedly did not miss a single assignment during twenty-seven seasons in the Southern Association—more than 4400 games.[5] He officiated ten Dixie World Series pitting the champion of the Southern Association against the winner of the Texas League, and officiated every Southern all-star game from the inception of the contest in 1938 through his retirement in 1946. Steamboat only knows how many no-hitters he called. He worked with some seventy umpires while in the Southern Asociation alone, mentored most of them, and saw eight promoted to the majors.[6] Already a living legend in 1935, Johnson ensured his place in baseball history by the unprecedented act of publishing *Standing the Gaff*.

I

In writing the first book-length life of an umpire, Johnson scooped the field by eighteen years and remains the lone umpire to publish his own autobiography.[7] Atlanta sports editor Ed Danforth, who originally suggested that Johnson write an autobiography, intended only a magazine article, but "the Steamer," as usual, had a more grandiose vision.[8] Suddenly taking up the pen during the 1935 season, Steamboat within weeks wrote a book-length manuscript on hotel stationery. And because a self-written umpire's autobiography had limited commercial value, especially in the middle of the Great

Depression, he got a graphic artist to design the dust jacket, and arranged for its publication. Advertising helped defray the cost of printing, but without a distributor, he had to sell copies by hawking them at ballparks before games and filling personal orders.[9] He took out ads in *The Sporting News,* where the book received a favorable review: "Few fans would think of sitting up half the night with an umpire unless it was at a wake, but if they start reading Johnson's book, they won't put it down until they have completed it."[10] However, the book engendered more publicity than sales, and Steamboat always maintained that he lost money on the venture.[11]

Why did he forego the literary assistance of the sportswriter who had given him his trademark nickname and privately publish the book? *Standing the Gaff* is truly a vanity production, a testimonial to Johnson's consuming ego. Umpires, by personality and profession, traditionally shun the spotlight, but Steamboat, ever the exception to the rule, craved public attention. With Bill Brennan's retirement in 1933, Johnson was both the senior umpire in the Southern Association and the dean of minor league umpires. Writing his autobiography was another means of obtaining recognition; within months after it appeared, he bought, presumably not from royalties, a ring in the shape of a baseball and inscribed with a diamond and an umpire's indicator.[12] More specifically, Johnson may have decided to publish his memoirs in response to the widespread criticism of Southern arbiters during the 1935 season.[13]

The circumstances of the book's publication account for its rough edges. Writing hurriedly, almost in steam-of-consciousness fashion, Johnson did not always bother to provide complete names, dates of events, or adequate explanations. He assumed readers would be knowledgeable fans and thus understand off-hand references to people and events. Didn't everyone know that the Western League was called "101 Ranch" after the Miller brothers' 101 Ranch Wild West Show?[14] Although Johnson did not check his remembrance of things past with contemporary records, there are remarkably few errors, none of major consequence.[15] On the other hand, that the book was self-produced accounts for much of its charm and value: *Standing the Gaff* is a credible chronicle wherein Johnson recorded 'em as he remembered 'em, instead of consciously manufacturing. If his memory is not always exact and his recollections sometimes embellished, the stories are correct in essentials. Like all autobiographies, the book is important not only for what things he remembered, but also how he remembered them; not only for what he included, but also for what he omitted. Steamboat's anecdotes are interesting and amusing, but his book is more than the sum of its parts: it is a compelling portrait of the life and hard times of a minor league umpire.

Standing the Gaff is less an autobiography than a career chronicle. Were it not for Ed Danforth's prodding, the book would contain virtually no information about Johnson's family or personal life. (The lone exception, a detailed account of his brother Joseph's murder, indicates its traumatic effect on his life.)[16] Unfortunately, subsequent research has produced little new information about his personal life. We now know that his given name probably was Henry, that he was born on March 26, 1884, to Samuel and Rosalia Steinfield Johnson, and that his father was an Irish Catholic and his mother was a German Jew.[17] A prominent sandlot first baseman, he reportedly turned down a contract to play for Danville with the Class D Virginia–North Carolina League in 1905 because his father thought baseball was "too uncouth and rowdy a profession."[18] The date he and Bertha Miller wed remains uncertain, but it was likely in 1918.[19] Marriage apparently brought Johnson into a close-knit family, for he lived in his wife's hometown, Ionia, Michigan, for most of the years from 1918 to 1925.[20] It was undoubtedly easier for the couple to endure Steamer's life-long career in an occupation that was notoriously hard on family life because they were childless. They adopted late in life a son,

Tommy.[21] Like all umpires, Johnson found it necessary to supplement his income with off-season employment, but he always sought work that would keep him in contact with the public. During the 1920s he was an assistant manager of a Memphis department store, and in the 1930s operated a cafe, Steamboat Johnson's Eat Shoppe. By 1942 he was a field representative for the Wilson Truck Company, making public relations appearances through the South, and then sold ballpark lighting equipment. He maintained a close association with sport, for years refereeing boxing matches in the Memphis area; and through friendship with Memphis Bill Terry, manager of the New York Giants from 1932 to 1941, umpired the team's spring exhibition games. A Shriner and a Thirty-second Degree Mason, Johnson was involved in numerous community projects.

Extroverted and garrulous in public, Johnson was in truth an intensely private man. Only impending death prompted him to reveal his most closely guarded personal secret: from his hospital deathbed, he sent for a rabbi and declared his Jewish faith. When the rabbi expressed surprise because Johnson had never attended synagogue or associated with the sizable Jewish community in Memphis, Steamboat confessed that he concealed his religion because he feared anti-Semitic taunts: "It's bad enough being an umpire, but to be a Jew, too, would have been terrible."[22]

Johnson wrote *Standing the Gaff* mindful of literary and social conventions and of his status as an active umpire. In Steamboat's day, sports personalities were cast as role models, or at least influential cultural icons, and their "life stories," whether appearing in books or periodicals, were invariably positive and inspirational stories of achievement. Thus, Johnson recounts numerous nasty and violent confrontations with players and fans without vulgar detail. "What the players say to us and what we say in return cannot be set down in this book," he intoned with juridical discretion. He also wrote as a gentleman, keenly aware of social propriety. Thus he says only nice things about people, even the dyspeptic John McGraw, one of the most shamelessly vicious umpire baiters of all time. (The treatment of McGraw is ironic in that the Giants manager likely played a significant role in his dismissal from the National League.) The social temper of the times precluded discussion of race, concerning either the popularity of Negro League baseball and black barnstormers or the segregation in distant bleachers of the large numbers of blacks who attended "white" league and exhibition games. Yet Steamboat was acutely aware of segregation: when umpiring on the bases he often would "go out into the negro [sic] bleacher section, and bark the batteries in a tone that only Johnson could, and would always get a big hand."[23]

As an employee of the Southern Association, Steamboat wrote with restraint about umpires and umpiring. There are few objective standards by which to distinguish the abilities of umpires, so job security for arbiters has always depended on the whim of league presidents who themselves are controlled by team owners. Umpires had to get along or get on, and Johnson demonstrates throughout *Standing the Gaff* that he was a strong "company man" who understood the public relations aspect of his job. Thus he did not discuss the business side of professional umpiring—the meager salaries and per diem allowances, the inadequate (or nonexistent) facilities at ballparks, the lack of pension programs and health insurance, or the contractual "reserve clause" that bound umpires to leagues like players were bound to teams. Such things, he believed, were matters for private negotiation, not public discussion. Similarly, he knew that not all arbiters lived lives "as isolated as a monk in a monastery," and that many promising careers crashed in life's fast lane. But his sense of propriety as well as his status as an active umpire precluded mentioning the boozing, wenching, and gambling so rampant among all participants in the game. If Johnson's comments on the character and deportment of umpires seem old-fashioned at best, hopelessly idealistic at worst, they nonetheless speak to the expectations that obtained in 1935. After all, contemporaries viewed Steamboat not as a quaint character but as the quintessential umpire. And while conveying a strong sense of umpire camaraderie and the "we-they" perspective of embattled crews, Johnson has little to say about other umpires with whom he worked, and virtually nothing about those who reached the majors. That he commented mostly on those who had brief stays in the league while ignoring the likes of Bill McGowan, a future Hall of Fame arbiter, suggests his identification with those who, like himself, served well but never advanced, as well as his lingering resentment over his failure to return to the majors.

To Johnson, umpiring—despite poor salaries, miserable working conditions, and constant abuse—was a noble calling. His address at the annual meeting of minor league officials in Louisville in 1922 is eloquent testimony to his devotion to the profession. Johnson reportedly worked thirty days on a twenty-minute address that was both timely in its plea for greater support for umpires and timeless in its discussion of the seemingly elementary but essential attributes of the successful arbiter. There is no gainsaying his basic premise: at any given time, the umpire is the most important participant in a baseball game. His attack on "rhubarbs" was especially telling. Although physical abuse of professional umpires has virtually ceased, on-field verbal assaults continue: baseball is the only sport that allows participants to argue at length with officials about judgment calls during the course of a game.[24] According to *The Sporting News*, the "rattling good talk" put club owners and league administrators "on the pan pretty severely for their part in encouraging rowdyism," but "what he said was 100 per cent true and his squirming hearers, knowing it, took his 'decisions' without talking back."[25] Small wonder that Commissioner Kenesaw Mountain Landis called Johnson's speech "the best exposition ever put together on the profession of umpiring" and requested a copy for his files.[26]

Johnson probably intended the book to end with the reprinting of his famous speech inasmuch as the last three chapters appear to be afterthoughts. The listing of players who made the major leagues and sampling of "knotty rules problems" are conventional inclusions to enhance sales, while the discussion of the Goldsmith baseball is transparent acknowledgment of the company's multiple ads that helped underwrite the publication of the book. However, his promotion of the Association of Professional Ball Players of America was wholly altruistic. Johnson, who joined the APBPA in 1927, three years after its founding in 1924, and Clarence "Pants" Rowland, former player and manager who umpired in the American League, were the two leading champions of the organization among umpires. Apart from his conviction that umpires should be prominent members of the professional baseball fraternity, Steamboat believed deeply in the organization's assistance programs.[27] Not surprisingly, he regarded umpiring one of the numerous APBPA benefit games as one of his "most prized assignments."[28]

Standing the Gaff is a classic of baseball literature. Steamboat was a born raconteur, quick to tell tales tall and true at a moment's lull in the conversation, and the book is full of wonderful anecdotes. That Johnson chose not to reminisce about the numerous memorable player performances he had witnessed—Johnny Bates hitting safely in 46 consecutive games in 1915, Jim Poole clubbing 50 homers and 167 RBIs in 1930, and Phil Winetraub batting .401 in 1934—and instead record only his recollections of umpires and umpiring speaks volumes as to his single-minded devotion to the profession. Parts of the book are timeless: Johnson's prescriptions for good umpiring, condemnation of senseless arguments, concern for the integrity of the game, and interest in speedily played contests are as relevant today as in 1935. But it is especially valuable as a period piece, an intimate look at the inglorious life of an umpire during the glory days of baseball—the techniques and equipment, the travel and loneliness, the routines and rhubarbs. Steamer began umpiring during the early days of the National Association of Professional Baseball Clubs, a cartel created in 1901 to bring administrative and economic stability to the minor leagues. Like the game itself, he struggled through the dislocations of World War I, blossomed during the Golden Age of the 1920s, survived the hardships of the depression and World War II, and enjoyed peak popularity by mid-century. Over the course of thirty-seven years Steamboat Johnson had witnessed the social, economic, and political forces that transformed baseball from national pastime to big business, and umpiring from hazardous job to reputable career.[29]

II

When Johnson took up the indicator, it was the best and worst of times for an aspiring umpire. The National Agreement combined with a booming economy to create a heyday for minor league baseball. In 1910, when Johnson at age twenty-six signed his first professional contract, fifty-two leagues were in operation. There were lots of opportunities for umpires, but getting a job was difficult. There were no umpiring schools to provide formal training, no supervisors to instruct and facilitate career advancement: umpires learned their trade by calling 'em in local amateur or semipro games. Politics and personalities more than ability were the keys to getting and keeping a job. Johnson became a professional umpire because Pittsburgh sports editor Richard Guy recommended him to George L. Moreland, president of the Class C Ohio-Pennsylvania League, which save for Erie, Pennsylvania, was an eastern Ohio circuit. He advanced the next year to Class A after coworker and fellow umpire John Mullin put in a good word for him with Norris L. "Tip" O'Neill, president of the Western League, a far-flung circuit extending from Des Moines to

Denver and featuring fans and players who exhibited a raucous and rowdy style reminiscent of the region's not-too-distant Wild West past. Released after the season, Johnson was on the verge of leaving umpiring when he met fellow-ump Steve Cusack, who got him a job in the Class B Three I League (Iowa, Illinois, Indiana) for 1913. Johnson's career changed dramatically when, at season's end, he boldly wrote to John K. Tener, president of the National League, requesting a job.[30]

Johnson wrote at a most opportune time. The National League staff was unsettled: Brick Owens and Bill Guthrie had been dismissed, Bill Brennan had jumped to the new Federal League as umpire-in-chief, and in early February 1914 veteran Hank O'Day unexpectedly resigned to become manager of the Chicago Cubs. Desperately needing a new umpire, Tener promptly signed Johnson as O'Day's replacement. However, his place on the eight-man regular staff was short-lived. When the league in April signed William F. "Bill" Hart of the Southern Association, an ex-major league pitcher who happened to be a former teammate of Tener's, Johnson joined newcomers Frederick Lincoln and Arthur O'Connor on the substitute list.[31]

Johnson umpired fifty-four games in the major leagues. He debuted on April 26 in Cincinnati, joining Ernie Quigley as a replacement for the ill Mal Eason. His next game was June 25 in Philadelphia. Al Orth tore a ligament in his leg after slipping on the concrete at the front of the player's dugout, and while Orth hobbled on crutches, Johnson for the next six weeks teamed with second-year man Bill Byron. They accompanied Boston's "Miracle Braves" on the western swing around the league that launched their unprecedented drive from last place on the Fourth of July to the championship. They also called the record-setting twenty-one-inning game between the New York Giants and Pittsburgh on July 17, a game that was unsuccessfully protested by the Pirates because of a call by Byron.[32]

A series between Cincinnati and the Giants at the Polo Ground likely proved crucial in determining Johnson's future in the league. The series began on July 30, and Johnson, who was umpiring the bases, in the ninth inning ejected in quick succession four Giants—Mike Donlin, manager John McGraw, Fred Snodgrass, and Albie Fletcher. He tossed McGraw again the next day, and during the third contest engaged in an embarrassingly long discussion with Byron as to what to do about two Reds who wound up simultaneously at second base. Then, during the series-ending doubleheader, Byron chased McGraw and Snodgrass, and after the game the umps left the field under a barrage of bottles.[33] An incensed McGraw went public with a scathing criticism of the league's umpires, identifying Byron ("ignorantly arrogant") and Johnson ("deficient in knowledge of the rules") as the worst of the bunch. Replaced by Lincoln on August 12, Johnson ended his tour of duty with a bang, tossing hometown Philadelphia favorite, Hans Lobert, for "kicking."[34]

Johnson made only token appearances the rest of the season. When Billy Hart suddenly took ill during a doubleheader between Cincinnati and Brooklyn on September 21, Johnson, who happened to be in the stands, worked the second game. He also worked the next day's game with Cy Rigler, and then joined Byron on October 1 for a season-ending five-game set between the Reds and the Pirates.[35]

Johnson's high hopes for the 1915 season were dashed in December when he learned that his contract would not be renewed. He thought his assignment to umpire the annual postseason exhibition series in St. Louis between the Browns and Cardinals was a reward for a job well done, when in fact it was either a final test or the umpire's equivalent of severance pay.[36] (The contract of his partner in the city series, the rookie American League umpire Joseph O'Brien, was also not renewed for 1915.) The more significant indicator of his performance is that his only non-emergency assignment of the year was a meaningless season's finale between the league's two worst teams.

For the rest of his life Johnson was confused and embittered by his failure to return to the majors. What went wrong in 1914 and, more important, why was Johnson not recalled after more seasoning in the minors? In part, Johnson was victimized by the National League's revolving-door policy. In contrast to the American League's stable corps of umpires, the senior circuit for several years prior to World War I annually hired several new, and often inexperienced, umpires only to release them at season's end. Of the four new umpires signed for 1914, Hart alone "gave satisfaction" and was retained.[37]

League umpires had been roundly criticized during the season, especially by McGraw and Boston manager George Stallings. By August, President Tener was forced to reprimand McGraw, ordering him to "lay off" public criticism of the umpiring.[38] But a *Sporting News* editorial of August 6 echoed McGraw's criticism of "certain newcomers," focusing on "one hair trigger sort of an arbiter who was a whole lot more absorbed in sending players to the club house than he was gauging balls and strikes" and adding that his "work on balls and strikes was not good." Most telling, John B. Foster, secretary of the Giants, railed editorially in the league's official guide book against the poor umpiring of the 1914 season, calling it "the worst year of umpiring . . . in a long time." Thinking the problem was "not so much with the veterans" as with the newcomers, Foster charged:

> "At least one of the more recent appointees was too much of a buffoon to succeed in a task which calls for so much dignity as that of umpire in a national organization of sport. One of the experiments [appointments] was experimental to the effect that he unconsciously, by wretched judgment, began the change of atmosphere which fell to the lot of the league. A third umpire, at least fifty times out of one hundred, gave a decision in advance of the play actually being made, and by the over-officiousness destroyed his usefulness exactly as much as it would have been impaired by lack of official judgment. . . . The umpire, who, like one of the

> National League staff of 1914, exploits his greatness as an umpire before his fellow-umpires and before friends and the public generally, is hardly of the caliber which should be selected. His was the tendency to make his position a farce and his organization a joke.[39]

It is not known which of Foster's criticism were directed at Johnson, but it seems likely that, whatever the technical quality of his work, the major leagues were not ready for his flamboyant style of umpiring. When Johnson developed his "colorful" style is unknown, but it was evident by the time he reached the Western League, where reporters described him as an umpire with an "artistic temperament" who "objects to language which borders on the rude."[40] He changed leagues, but not deportment in 1913. Johnson's decisive call in the Quincy-Dubuque game (p. 30) may have outraged the hometown fans less because it cost their team the pennant than because of his antics. He reportedly "started to dance on his toes up-and-down" as the play developed and wound up badly out of position to make the call: "He was between home and the pitcher's box by the time the play ended, and must have been so interested in his terpsichorean effort that he forgot to watch the play."[41] Working with Bill Byron in 1914 did not help. Byron, who had come up in 1913 and was well on the way to earning the sobriquet "Lord Byron" for his habit of accompanying calls with sing-song verse, was a poor role model. Byron concluded the season by working his first World Series, but it would be his last autumn classic; displeasure with his theatrics mounted, and he was released after the 1919 season. Although Johnson admitted in *Standing the Gaff* that he "learned a lot about umpiring" during the subsequent three years spent in the New York State League, his inability (refusal?) to change his on-field demeanor cost him a major league career.

Johnson was devastated. His disappointment was so great that twenty years later the only bitter comments contained in his memoirs were those directed toward his brother's murderer and his replacement in the National League, George Cockill, who "never umpired."[42] His partner in the St. Louis series, Joe O'Brien, and former colleague, John Mullin, joined the Federal League for 1915, but Johnson, whether for fear of jeopardizing a possible recall to the National League or because his style of umpiring was not acceptable even to the new circuit, swallowed his pride and signed on with the Class B New York State League.

It was a pleasure to be back in Elmira and the other central New York towns of his youth, but the outbreak of World War I brought hard times to baseball and its umpires. Declining attendance, manpower shortages, and travel restrictions led to the imposition of severe cost-cutting measures and the suspension of operations by clubs and leagues. The 1914 season opened with forty-four leagues, but only twenty-one remained by 1917. Johnson endured the hardships, honed his umpiring skills, and followed league president John H. Farrell to the International League in 1918. It was the worst year in the history of minor league baseball. Ten leagues started, but the International League alone finished the season; in fact, it was the only circuit to last beyond July 22.[43] The Steamer had survived and, having at last reached the highest classification in the minor leagues (AA), anticipated soon returning to the majors. Instead, he was released when David Fultz became president of the league at season's end.

Recently married and tired of disappointments, Johnson at age thirty-five began to pursue employment opportunities outside of baseball. But he changed his mind when Judge John D. Martin, newly appointed president of the Southern Association, offered him a job on the recommendation of Mike Finn, old-time player, manager, and scout. The coming of peace in 1919 ushered in baseball's Golden Age, but instead of riding the wave of popularity back to the majors, Johnson found himself sailing down the Mississippi to Memphis and a rendezvous with destiny in the Southern Association.

The Southern Association, popularly known as the Southern League, was one of minor league baseball's premier organizations.[44] Throughout its sixty-year history, the Southern operated as the second highest classification in the minors.[45] Encompassing the largest and most cosmopolitan cities in the region, it developed into one of the minor's most stable and administratively efficient leagues; six of the eight charter members of 1901 remained in the league for a half century or more. Capitalizing on the strong fan support and a salubrious climate that made Dixie the home of major league baseball's spring training as well as a host of professional and semiprofessional leagues, the Southern, under the aggressive leadership of Martin, was at the forefront of the minor league baseball boom of the 1920s that saw thirty leagues in operation by 1928. Adding to fan interest was the advent of the farm system in 1921, whereby major league clubs owned minor league teams, and the expansion of the Negro National League into the South with franchises in Birmingham, Memphis, and Nashville.

Ex-major leaguer Bill Brennan and veteran Southern arbiter Dan Pfenninger headed the staff, but Steamboat Johnson immediately became the most talked-about umpire in the league. He opened the season with the Memphis Chicks and the Little Rock Travelers; the latter club was managed by the fiery Kid Elberfeld, long the league's holy terror.[46] The initial game in Little Rock on April 24 featured only routine carping, as did the second contest, played in Memphis. But in the third contest, also played in Memphis, Johnson tossed Elberfeld and had him escorted by police out of the park. The next day Johnson again tossed the Kid and banished him from the park after Elberfeld reportedly grabbed the umpire's coattails and threatened to hit him. President Martin promptly suspended Elberfeld, and the Little Rock papers mercilessly roasted Johnson, calling him a "comedian" and "czar," a "very poor" umpire who had "many bad guesses on balls and strikes," and a man who carried a "grudge" against Elberfeld and the Travelers. It was an inauspicious debut: in his first six games, Johnson tossed two managers and fined five players, and the press thought his umpiring was "anything but wonderful."[47]

Amid growing criticism of league umpiring, which saw two arbiters quit and a third threaten to resign, Johnson's reputation was reborn in Atlanta. Following his initial appearance in mid-June, the press enthused that he was "the feature of the game," a "personality" whose "originality" in umpiring should win "the blue ribbon." He was found to be "a hard worker and a sincere, conscientious fellow" who "follows the ball like a hawk, keeps the game going along at a fast clip and puts pep and life into the player and the fans." He was also found to be entertaining. When Nashville changed pitchers, Johnson not only announced the new pitcher, but also spelled his name! That gimmick won him "friends galore in the press box" with the announcement, and "from then on [he] had the crowd by both hands. He could have called every ball a strike and gotten away with it." Fans also delighted in his antics: "Mr. Johnson, every two or three innings, has one of the players to wash his eyes out with a certain substance so that his vision will remain bright and accurate." As the *Atlanta Constitution* put it: "There have been umpires and just plain umps, boobs and scientific decision announcers at Ponce de Leon park, but until Monday afternoon Atlanta had never been honored by such an umpire as the one which put in appearance in the person of Henry S. Johnson."[48] Johnson subsequently did nothing to diminish his reputation as "a humdinger," and a week later the *Journal* exclaimed: "Johnson is one of the best umpires we have seen . . . but he certainly missed his calling when he did not go on the stage as a comedian."[49]

Johnson's march on Atlanta also resulted in a new nickname and persona. Early in his umpiring career he had been nicknamed Bulldog. In the foreword to *Standing the Gaff*, Ed Danforth (and presumably Johnson) said the monicker stemmed from a "pugnacious disposition and his willingness to engage in a fight on the slightest provocation." All other explanations refer not to his bark, but to his habit of using his teeth to open boxes of new baseballs.[50] But Atlantans were struck by his resonant voice. "When he announces the batteries he reaches far down into his lungs and sweeps his voice all around the stands," reported the *Journal*. "He twists his mouth and gesticulates like a Fourth of July orator delighting the multitudes from the elevation of a soap box." *Georgian* sports editor Ed Danforth was so taken he opined that the "S" in Johnson's name "probably stands for 'steamboat'" because "the old boy had a voice like a Lee line packet in distress."[51] From then on he was "Steamboat" to Danforth and to everyone else, for Johnson not only embraced the new moniker, but also added a windmill motion to his calls to accentuate the paddlewheeler image.[52]

Johnson's most important game may have been the marathon twenty-three-inning 2–2 tie between the Lookouts and Atlanta in Chattanooga on June 13. Although called because of darkness, the longest game in Southern Association history took only three hours and forty minutes to play, in large measure because Johnson, demonstrating his ability to run a game, kept players hustling by urging them to "hurry it up, boys." He also proved his mettle in the bottom of the nineteenth inning when a Chattanooga batter singled with the bases loaded and two out. As the apparent winning run crossed the plate, the runner at first base committed a bush-league version of Fred Merkle's famous boner by leaving the field before touching second. When the Crackers alertly threw the ball to the keystone bag, Johnson called the runner out and disallowed the run. It was a tough call to make against the home team, and it was tribute to Johnson's performance that "nobody kicked."[53]

Despite unbridled success in the Southern, Johnson bolted at the end of his second season to the South Atlantic League because of "salary inducements" proffered by the Class B circuit.[54]

It could have been a career-ending mistake for the thirty-eight-year-old arbiter. Johnson quickly regretted his decision, and after "a long talk" with Judge Martin returned to the Southern for 1922. While Steamer does not discuss in *Standing the Gaff* why he switched leagues in 1921 or the conditions of his return, perhaps it is enough to note that he dedicated the book to Martin, to whom he owed his career.

Over the next twenty-five years, Johnson flourished in the Southern Association. The Steamer and the Southern were made for each other. The first minor league to institute "Ladies Day" and the "rain check," the Southern was always a leader in promotions; during the 1920s local owners like Joe Engel of Chattanooga, dubbed the "P. T. Barnum of Baseball," competed to devise new gimmicks to attract fans. Steamboat's performance on the field complemented the entertainment planned by the front offices, and he quickly became the top draw in the league. He was so popular that local newspapers advertised his scheduled arrival days in advance of the games. Ironically, the style of umpiring that kept Steamer from the majors was his ticket to success in the minors.

His signature feature was the basso profundo voice that so recalled a riverboat's steam whistle as to inspire his nickname. Asked why he bellowed his calls so loudly, the Steamer explained: "I want the fellows in the cheap seats to hear whether it's a ball or a strike."[55] Reports that people in Memphis could "follow a Johnson-umped game in Atlanta simply by raising the window" are unsubstantiated, but there is no denying that many fans arrived early so as to be sure to hear him announce the batteries (actually, baaaaterrreeeees) at start of the game.[56] Most umpires used a megaphone to project their voices, but Steamer unleashed a voice that reverberated throughout the field. "I always thought that the advent of the public address system in ball parks was Steamer's saddest day," mused sportswriter Freddy Russell.[57]

But it was his conduct on the field that made him a favorite in press box and bleachers. Johnson's exaggerated motions, florid forensics, and comedic antics both entertained and drew fans. Watching him umpire was worth the price of admission. Steamboat working behind the bat was itself grand entertainment. He brushed home plate "with the flurry of a fox terrior digging out a mole." He "rode" conspicuously with the pitch—going down for low balls and stretching up for high ones. His hands wiggled frantically when calling strikes. If he thought a baserunner might try for third, he would run full speed to the hot corner, then "prancing back to the plate, look up in the stands to note if the fans reacted to his super-hustle." Steamboat was only slightly less flamboyant when umpiring the bases. At the start of the game, he would sprint to his position down the first baseline, often continuing well into the outfield where he would announce the pitchers and catchers to the bleacher folk. "Safe" and "out" calls were made with exaggerated gestures and, ever hustling, he raced closely after base runners in order to be on top of the play.[58]

Steamboat's most famous antic derived from sensitivity about his eyesight. Players and fans alike traditionally have questioned the umpire's vision with charges ranging from visual impairment to outright blindness. Soon after joining the Southern Association, Johnson obtained an eye exam from an optometrist, had the certificate attesting to 20–20 vision notarized, and with feigned indignation showed the authentication of perfect vision to anyone who questioned his eyesight. He always held the certificate in such a way as to obscure the date of the examination. Cynical suggestions that he had worn out numerous photocopies over the years did nothing to diminish the effectiveness of his one-upmanship.[59]

"Steamer stories" became staples of baseball banter, moving into the realm of folk tales as they were repeated with growing embellishments. A favorite story involved one of Steamboat's greatest rhetorical triumphs. One day in Chattanooga (or Mobile, or Nashville), "in a box pressing hard upon the plate sat a celebrated surgeon who made a hobby of operating upon the Steamer without the use of anesthetics. Voice scalpel-sharp this day, he pressed the attack right lustily until at last the umpire threw up his arms and called time—stalked to the netting [and] in tones which rebounded from Lookout Mountain" asked the physician if he knew the difference between a doctor and an umpire. When the doctor pleaded ignorance, Johnson intoned: "Well, a doctor has an undertaker to cover his mistakes, and umpires don't. When you make a mistake, it is buried and forgotten. When I make one, it lives forever. Play ball."[60]

Some tales were true, others tall. One of the most popular of the latter variety involved a Western League game in Denver (or Oklahoma City) in 1912. With the bases loaded in the bottom of the ninth of a tied game, a batter lofted a high fly to right field. As the fielder prepared to make the final out, some playful cowboys sitting (or standing) along the foul line drew their six-guns and blew the ball to bits. Three (or four) runs scored to win the game. The visiting club protested to no avail. Said Steamboat: "It was a home run, because the ball had disappeared from my view, having been shot into small pieces by the accurate aim of the cowboys." He chortled, "That was one play I did not call against the home team."[61]

As the ego so apparent in *Standing the Gaff* suggests, it was not by happenstance that Johnson occupied center stage. A thespian at heart, he made sure no one could overlook his presence on the field. He enjoyed both cheers and jeers. It mattered not that some adored him and others abhorred him, so long as none ignored him. As old friend Fred Russell, sports editor of the *Nashville Banner* put it: "Steamer possessed a stage presence and he exercised it to the fullest."[62] He relished the attention, and it was monumental understatement to say that Steamboat "took delight in listening to the cheers."[63]

Johnson's showmanship was partly a calculated attempt to defuse tense situations with humor and partly a natural expression of his personality, although it is impossible to determine the proportions. One scribe felt that Steamboat didn't "really mean to put on most of his acts; I think it was just his nature to put lots of pep into his work and to see the humorous side of things. Anyhow, he furnished lots of amusement at times, and, at times, the sideshow helped you sit through a one-side, long-drawn-out game."[64] There is no denying the genuineness of his trademark gestures: on opening day each year, he always shook hands with the league veterans, welcoming them back for another season, and after the final out in the last game of the year, he always turned to the fans and shouted "God Bless You." [65]

For all the attention given his showmanship, Johnson enjoyed a long and successful career because he was a very good umpire. After all, nice guys finish last and likable folks get fired. Sportswriters knew that Steamer "appreciated the fact that there was a discerning crowd at his back," but agreed that he did not sacrifice good judgment for the sake of theatrics and that he worked "desperately hard at his profession, and was dauntless in the clutch."[66] Sportswriters were not alone in thinking that Johnson "in his prime was truly a good umpire."[67] Fresco Thompson, a nine-year major league player who later managed the New Orleans Pelicans, declared: "He's a showboat as well as a steamboat. But umpires don't come any better. He's firm in his decisions and his eyesight is perfect."[68] Judge Martin, who initially was uneasy about Johnson's reputation, later admitted: "Johnson was a very fine umpire, with all his color."[69]

His personality and demeanor made him a very popular umpire, but what made him a proficient umpire was his ability to run a game, his courage, and his integrity. Johnson was neither a tough, cop-on-the-beat enforcer like the National League's Bill Klem nor a soft-spoken, diplomatic adjudicator like the American League's Tommy Connolly. He had a unique style of running the game, combining firmness and fairness with a healthy dose of good humor to garner affection as well as respect. Players also admired his hustle. He drove himself and ball clubs with "fierce intensity," and under his direction "games were played at a rolling gallop."[70] He also had that invaluable intangible quality called "presence." He carried himself with an air of assurance born of confidence, not arrogance. Steamboat was good, and he knew it. Good judgment, handling situations and making calls correctly, is an umpire's most important skill. Steamboat was a careful student of human nature, and could handle people as well as an indicator. He understood the competitive passions of players and managers, and thus set his pressure-gauge on low. It was hard to get the Steamer's boiler to over-heat, but when it did there was no doubting that he was "lord and master on the diamond. There was fire in his eyes, a retort on his lips, and purposefulness expressed in his swimming gait. When he turned his back on a player or manager, folded his arms, and set to shaking his head from side to side in a no-no-no expression, fans knew something was about to pop. When he pulled his watch and started counting the minutes, someone was headed for a shower."[71]

A conspicuous theme of Johnson's aptly-named memoir is courage—not only the resolve to make tough calls, but also the rectitude necessary to stand the gaff. Umpires have long been the most vilified of sports officials. Baseball is the only game to ritualize verbal taunts from the stands and to sanction on-field rhubarbs. Words are injurious, but bottles and fists hurt. Whereas modern players and managers are automatically fined and suspended if they bump the ump, Johnson worked in an era when "Kill the Umpire" was no mere rhetorical threat. He and his fellow arbiters faced physical danger every time they walked onto the diamond. They were beaten with fists, bombarded with flying glassware, and threatened, on occasion even assaulted, with lethal weapons. Homicides were not unknown. Major league umpires were not immune from violence; future Hall of Famer Billy Evans was nearly killed after being skulled by a pop bottle in 1907 and was beaten savagely by Ty Cobb in 1921. But as *Standing the Gaff* amply illustrates, brawling and bottle tossing, not to mention vilification, became fine arts in the minors, giving new meaning to the term "bush league." It took guts to endure the abuse. At the end of his career, Johnson's head was covered with "pop bottle souvenirs," but he proudly maintained: "Every scar I've got is the result of an honest decision."[72]

Integrity was the hallmark of his career. To Steamboat, an umpire's integrity turned not only on making honest decisions and impartially enforcing the rules, but also on maintaining proper appearances, ranging from personal habits to fraternizing with players and fans. He proudly tells of tossing Ty Cobb, who had hired him to umpire Detroit's spring games, from an exhibition when the fans would eagerly have forgiven laxity in exchange for seeing the Georgia Peach play.[73] (Johnson's partner, Cy Pfirman, was a new member of the National League staff; Steamboat must have enjoyed the delicious irony of a career minor leaguer upstaging the major leaguer.)

As illustrated by his encounter with gamblers in Denver in 1912, Johnson began umpiring during an era in which gambling on baseball was rampant; crooked players and fixed games were an open secret. Honesty was the one subject about which he could not joke. He did not find it amusing when sportswriters kidded him about his claim to 20/20 eyesight: "Don't ever show that card again, Steamer; let 'em think you're blind; that card might prove you're dishonest." He bristled at the notion of a dishonest ump, and said of the infamous Black Sox Scandal of 1919: "When the gamblers went out to fix a world's series, they did not try to make a deal with the umpires. They knew the umpires would turn them down . . . and in."[74] He was enormously proud of the honesty of his profession, and would have been disturbed to learn that his belief that no umpire in history had been charged with dishonesty was not true.[75]

As evidenced by his charmingly written autobiography,

Johnson was untutored but not unlettered. He worked hard to develop his verbal skills, both oral and written, perhaps as yet another way to impress people. His fascination with language led him to peruse dictionaries to discover uncommon or archaic terms, and he was prone to polysyllabic pomposity long before broadcaster Howard Cosell in the 1970s set new standards for elegant, if erroneous, use of multisyllable words. Nicholas "Red" Jones, who umpired with Johnson in the Southern from 1940 to 1943 before moving on to the American League for six seasons, delighted in telling stories about Steamboat's forensic faux pas:

"He was telling me (for the fiftieth time) about the day he stood on the base in New Orleans facing the bleachers and looked right down their throats as they threw bottles at him. 'The bottles were flying all around my head,' growled Steamboat. 'They didn't scare me. I stuck out my chin and looked right into the stands. I tell you, that took sheer saponified courage.' "

"So I went to a dictionary and looked up 'saponified.' It means 'converted to soap; soft, slippery, soapy.' I still use that one on him when he gets tough." Steamer never admitted the verbal miscue, but instead berated his partner for not appreciating linguistic lyricism.[76]

Umpiring was Johnson's first love, and giving a speech was his second. In great demand as a speaker, he relished the opportunity to display rhetorical pyrotechnics. When one of the league clubs asked him to present a watch to its most valuable player as determined by popular vote of the fans, Steamboat chugged through a dictionary and ended his presentation speech with an eloquent if egregious oratorical flurry:

"For conspicuous courage, for exceptional, unique and unusual ability, for your loyal subservience to team play, for your suave manner in addressing the umpires when you deemed it expedient to take issue with their ruling, even though at times your sardonic replies do not meet with the unqualified approval of the arbitrators, still it is the consensus of the men in blue that you richly deserve this gorgeous watch in approbation of your spectacular work in the field and at the bat." Nonplused, the player accepted the pocket watch and, noting that it did not have a chain, replied: "That was a helluva speech, Steamer, although I didn't understand very much of it. I want to say thanks to the fans—and, to you, you robber, where is the chain?"[77]

It is a tribute to the quality of Johnson's autobiography that readers want to know the rest of his story. After the book was published in December 1935, he stood the gaff for another eleven seasons and then served four years as supervisor of league umpires. It was a pivotal era for baseball. The Great Depression had a devastating impact on minor league baseball, reducing the number of operating leagues to fourteen in 1933. We would like to have his thoughts about the local promotions, including the Shaughnessy Playoffs, that helped baseball recover and grow to forty-four leagues by 1940. We would like to have his comments about the economic and manpower impact of World War II, in particular his views on Pete Gray, the one-armed outfielder who played for the Memphis Chicks in 1943 and 1944, and in the latter year was named the Association's Most Valuable Player. Formal umpire training schools were established by George Barr and Bill McGowan in 1935 and 1941, respectively, and we wonder not only about his evaluation of the boys in blue who graduated from schools instead of the sandlots, but also how he came to operate a school in 1950 in Kissimmee, Florida. Organized Baseball's racial barriers tumbled down when the Brooklyn Dodgers signed Jackie Robinson in 1946, and we would welcome his views on racial integration on major league spring training and minor league baseball in the South.

We do know that for the next fifteen years Steamboat Johnson was synonymous with minor league baseball umpiring. Apropos his national reputation, he was named umpire-in-chief for the National Association All-Star Game on July 9, 1939, at Cooperstown, New York, held as part of the ceremonies commemorating the founding of the National Baseball Hall of Fame. Not surprisingly, Steamboat "stole the show, his deep voice booming on every pitch, with such explanations as 'a great curve' or 'it's foul—I saw it myself from here,' keeping the crowd in stiches."[78]

It was a great honor, but secondary to that accorded him at the league's All-Star game in Nashville on July 9, 1943. The first umpire to be honored by the league for distinguished service, Johnson was showered with praise in pre-game ceremonies and then worked the plate as first-half champion Nashville defeated a league all-star team 3–2. President Billy Evans, former major league umpire, presented him with a pocket watch inscribed: "From the Southern Association to Harry (Steamboat) Johnson for 25 years of valiant service."[79] According to Red Jones, Steamer at the first opportunity rushed out to find a dictionary and returned to their hotel room "bursting with pride." "He said: 'Red, you see that word valiant? That's a great word, Red. It means vigorous in body, sturdy, powerful, stalwart, robust. It also means stout hearted, intrepid in danger and courageous. That's what they think of me, Red. To think that they could call me all those names during all those seasons, cry for my job and all that, and then give me a watch. Maybe they like me a little bit, after all." Ever the antagonist, Jones attempted to deflate Steamer's ego by pointing to the watch's trade-name and noting that "Omega" was at the end of the Greek alphabet. "That puts you pretty far down the list," he quipped. "No, Red," replied the Steamer, "it means I'll be with 'em until the finish."[80]

He was. His performance declined noticeably after 1940, and there was talk of putting Steamboat in dry dock when Evans became league president in 1943. Indeed, some thought that the All-Star game ceremony would be Johnson's farewell, but he was not about to walk away from the game he loved. After the conclusion of the 1946 season, Evans talked the loop's directors into creating the position of supervisor of umpires. Steamer, closing in on sixty-two years of age, was agreeable; on December 4 the league simultaneously announced his retirement as an active umpire and his appointment as umpire supervisor.[81]

In addition to observing and advising league umps, he earned his "handsome salary" by serving as a goodwill ambassador for the circuit, primarily by speaking to civic groups and youth organizations throughout the region. He especially enjoyed working with youngsters, instructing them on sportsmanship as well as baseball. He still had the urge to call 'em, and frequently umpired benefit games and youth games. From 1947 to 1950 he umpired the annual Nashville Junior League All-Star game sponsored by the *Tennessean,* and on one occasion traveled all night by bus to make the game. He was a regular at league functions, and "basked a bit in his past glory."[82]

His most memorable moment occurred on July 28, 1949, when New Orleans staged "Steamboat Johnson Night." Mayor De Lesseps S. Morrison and league president Charlie Hurth, former general managers of the Pelicans, joined forces to honor Steamer for forty years of service to organized ball and for his contributions to the New Orleans Recreation Department (NORD) youth baseball program. More than fifteen old-time players and umpires were on hand to pay tribute to the dean of minor league umpires. The evening began with a one-inning exhibition between two NORD teams, with the Steamer calling balls and strikes. When called to the field to accept his gifts, Steamboat appeared wearing dark glasses, led by a seeing-eye dog and handcuffed to a policeman. The ex-umps paid tribute to their brother in blue by roundly booing the fans. Johnson, who had balked at the idea of an "appreciation night," accepted the gifts and plaudits "with undisguised feelings which at times bordered on tears." In the league game that followed, the Pelicans defeated Steamboat's adopted hometown Memphis Chicks 9–3, a fitting finale for an umpire whose "fearless and impartial calling of plays made him anything but a 'homer.'"[83]

During his long and illustrious career, Steamboat's only regret—and it was huge—was not returning to major leagues. By 1925, when he and his wife moved to Memphis, thereby acknowledging a career commitment with the Southern Association, Johnson knew that he would never be recalled. He resolved to be biggest and best in the bushes, but never completely got over the disappointment. He undoubtedly envied the young umpires, like McGowan, who passed through the Southern en route to the majors, but found it even more frustrating to be stuck in the bushes while others who failed in their initial appearance in the big leagues were given a second chance.[84] At a certain point Johnson's advancing age precluded his call-up, but it was his "color" that had kept him out of the major leagues. John Heydler, former National League umpire who served as president of the Senior Circuit from 1918 to 1934 simply would not have accepted such a flamboyant arbiter. "If, as they say, old Canoe's over-developed sense of humor kept him out of the big leagues then the big leagues were the losers," opined Freddy Russell. "After turning him back they later were to welcome such clowns as [Larry] MacPhail, [Bill] Veeck and others."[85] More accurately, Steamer was ahead of his time, antedating by a half-century "colorful" umpires like Emmett Ashford, Ron Luciano, and Dutch Rennert.

Steamboat was often called the "Bill Klem of the minors" for more good reasons than people knew. Klem was the most famous of all major league umpires, Johnson the best in the minors. Supremely confident of his rectitude in making calls, The Old Arbitrator said; "I never missed one in my heart." Neither did the Steamer. Upon retiring in 1941, Klem became the first supervisor of National League umpires in this century; six years later, Johnson became the first to hold the position in the Southern Association. Honored on Bill Klem Day at New York's Polo Grounds on September 2, 1949, the future Hall of

Fame arbiter declared: "Baseball to me is not a game; it is a religion." Johnson, who had been similarly feted six weeks earlier in New Orleans, was of the same belief, but likely would have said: "Umpiring to me is not a profession; it is a religion." Both men were former first basemen who took up umpiring to stay in the game. Klem, who began his umpiring career in 1902 and was Johnson's early umpire idol, died at age seventy-seven from a heart attack on September 1, 1951, some six months after Johnson passed away.

Henry (Harry) Samuel Johnson died at age sixty-six in Memphis on February 20, 1951. He had been ill for more than a year, suffering from arteriosclerosis and diverticulosis of the colon, and had been hospitalized for almost a month when he suffered a fatal myocardial infarction following surgery. Incorrectly but fittingly, the death certificate gives his middle name as Steamboat. The monicker had become his identify, just as umpiring had become his life. According to long-time Memphis sportswriter George Lapidis: "Nobody knew him in his umpiring days as anything except 'Steamboat.' Most people couldn't have told you his first name."[86] Obituaries appeared in every daily paper in the Southern Association cities where he had umpired, and all but the *Atlanta Constitution* commented editorially on his career. With a florid flourish that would have delighted Steamboat, Walter Stewart, sports editor of the Memphis *Commercial Appeal*, eulogized his old friend as "a man of high professional skills, Gargantuan kindliness and astringent wit. . . . Colorful as a rocketing pheasant—thunder-throated and thirsty for stage's center, he brought drama into the ball park and played his lines with a right Falstaffian gusto." More succinct, but no less accurate, was his observation: "There was never a doubt concerning the burning sincerity of this man—his passionate attention to duty."[87] It is fitting, given Johnson's flair for the dramatic and fixation with language, that George Bugbee, sports editor of the *Memphis Press-Scimitar,* saluted Steamer's last trip around the bend in verse:[88]

Umpire's Epitaph

How does an umpire last so long—
Calling 'em right—calling 'em wrong?

Eggings and bottles are tough on the hide,
Cuss words and catcalls cut deep down inside.
Foul tips are murder to ankle and shin,
Foul language worse on the sered soul within:
Stormed at by players and stoned by the press,
Ridden by fans when he makes the wrong guess;
Friendless, forsaken—a social outcast,
How can a martyr like this hope to last?

Yet the "Steamer" had done it for 30-odd years,
Riding the tempest—sans anger, sans tears:
Keeping his courage, retaining his laugh,
Asking no quarter and "standing the gaff."

How does an umpire last so long?
"By calling 'em right, son—never one wrong."

Steamboat Johnson was one of a kind and one of the last of a kind. Given Organized Baseball's "up or out policy," whereby umpires are released if they fail to reach the majors within a prescribed timetable, there will never again be career minor league arbiters like the Steamer. While his long and highly successful career is remarkable, it raises questions as to why he chose to spend his life in the bushes, enduring the abuse and low pay, instead of moving on to more stable and productive occupation. *Standing the Gaff* provides no answers, but speaks volumes as to his sense of personal accomplishment, his hunger for public recognition, and his love of the game. Perhaps it is enough to know that his ability as an umpire, devotion to his profession, and unbridled humanity earned him the respect and affection of almost two generations of fans, players, managers, and sportswriters throughout the South. Fortunately, because he had the foresight and audacity to write an autobiography, future generations are also able to know and appreciate the Steamer.

NOTES

1. *The Sporting News*, February 28, 1951.

2. Unpublished feature story on Johnson by Emmett Maum (c. 1940), p. 10, *The Sporting News* Archives, St. Louis, Mo. I am indebted for this reference to Steven P. Gietschier, *TSN's* Director of Historical Records.

3. Interview with George Lapidis, Memphis, Tennessee, September 2, 1993.

4. Second to Johnson in minor league service is Ollie Anderson, who also umpired one year in the majors (Federal League 1914) and logged thirty-three years and some five thousand games in the minors.

5. Undated (1944) *New York Daily News* article, *TSN* Archives.

6. Steve Basil, Buck Campbell, Red Jones, Bill McGowan, and John Quinn advanced to the American League; Cy Pfirman, Edward McLaughlin, and James Scott to the National League.

7. Other book-length autobiographies are Babe Pinelli, as told to Joe King, *Mr. Ump* (Philadelphia: Westminster Press, 1953); Dusty Boggess, as told to Ernie Helm, *Kill the Ump!* (San Antonio: Lone Star Brewing Company, 1966); Jocko Conlan and Robert Creamer, *Jocko* (Philadelphia: J. B. Lippincott, 1967); Tom Gorman, as told to Jerome Holtzman, *Three and Two!* (New York: Charles Scribner's Sons, 1979); Ron Luciano and David Fisher, *The Umpire Strikes Back* (New York: Bantam Books, 1982), *Strike Two* (1984), *The Fall of the Roman Umpire* (1986), and *Remembrance of Swings Past* (1988); Dave Pallone, with Alan Steinberg, *Behind the Mask: My Double Life in Baseball* (New York: Viking, 1990); Eric Gregg and Marty Appel, *Working the Plate: The Eric Gregg Story* (New York: William Morrow, 1990); and Pam Postema and Gene Wojciechowski, *You've Got to Have Balls to Make It in This League: My Life as an Umpire* (New York: Simon & Schuster, 1992). Larry R. Gerlach, *The Men in Blue: Conversations with Umpires* (New York: Viking, 1980; reprinted University of Nebraska Press: Lincoln, 1994), is a collection of twelve umpire autobiographies.

8. *Atlanta Journal*, February 22, 1951. The extent of Danforth's contribution is unclear, but there is no reason to doubt his assertion that his role was that of editor, not ghost writer. The language and style of writing is vintage Johnson, while the missing details and partially developed material indicate amateur authorship.

9. There are numerous stories of Steamboat selling books before games began. Former minor league umpire Augie Guglielmo claimed to have been Johnson's partner the night he hawked books before a game in Memphis only to have fans, angered by one of his calls, throw books at him; Steamer supposedly picked them up and resold them in Nashville. Al Margulies, "'They Didn't Give Us Nothing,'" *Referee* (September 1993), 39. Guglielmo's story cannot be true because he umpired in the Southern only in 1949, three years after Johnson retired from active duty.

10. He ran two ads in *The Sporting News,* offering the hardback for $1.25 postpaid. Johnson was so well known that orders were to be sent to "Steamboat" Johnson, Umpire, Memphis, Tenn." *TSN*, December 19 and 26, 1935.

11. In 1944 he told sportswriter Jim McCully: "I buy the books and give them away myself. The darn thing has cost me $3,000 already. The book is just about in every part of the world today, and I guess I've bought every copy that was ever published. I get requests from all over the globe for the thing, but nobody ever wants to buy one." Undated (1944) *New York Daily News* article, *TSN* Archives.

12. Maum, unpub. MS., p. 10.

13. The umpiring staff underwent a major shakeup after the season, with more than half of the umpires replaced for 1936. See the Memphis *Commercial Appeal* and *Arkansas Democrat* (Little Rock), December 10, 1935.

14. Named after the family's 101 Ranch in Oklahoma, the show enjoyed national popularity from 1908 to 1916 with such featured performers as Tom Mix, Bill Pickett, and, for a time, Buffalo Bill Cody. See Collings Ellsworth and Alma Miller England, *The 101 Ranch* (Norman: University of Oklahoma Press, 1938).

15. Some of the errors are probably typographical: Burt Shotton, not Bert Shotten (p. 17); Mullin, not Mullen (p. 18); Cockill, not Cockrill (p. 38); Bluhm, not Blume (p. 80); Gleeson, not Gleason (p. 90); W. H. Walsh, not W. W. Walsh (p. 95, 97); Killefer, not Killifer (p. 130); Arvel, not Arnel Hall (p. 134); Alfonso, not Alphonse Lopez (p. 134); Myer, not Myers (p. 134); Newsom, not Newsome (p. 135); DeBerry, not Deberry (p. 136); and Ballanfant, not Ballafant (p. 136). Others were the result of slightly imprecise memory: it is Horace, not Howard Lisenbee (p. 134), and the record-setting game between the Giants and Pirates in 1914 lasted twenty-one, not twenty-two innings (p. 36). Sometimes the events of a few days are conflated on July 30. Johnson tossed John McGraw, Mike Donlin, Albie Fletcher, and Fred Snodgrass, not McGraw, Donlin, and Jeff Tesreau (p. 35); Cincinnati's pitcher was Leon "Red" Ames, not Larry Benton (John "Rube" Benton pitched the next day for the Reds), while Christy Mathewson, not Jeff Tesreau, pitched for the Giants (Tesreau was tossed later in the series). Only one error is baffling: John "Chief" Meyers ended his major league career in 1917 and thus already had been Christy Mathewson's catcher (p. 43), a strange slip-up because they were the battery in the July 30, 1914, game in which Johnson ejected several Giants.

16. The murder occurred on Sunday, June 9, not June 10. Johnson, who told reporters that he "will not rest until he has seen the slayer brought to justice," skipped the rest of the Denver–Des Moines series to help police try to identify the killer. The murder, part of a crime wave that terrorized Denver in

the summer of 1912, whipped the citizenry into a fury; a mob estimated at some two thousand persons chased and nearly lynched a suspect in the crime. When the investigation failed to produce an arrest, Johnson left town and resumed umpiring duties in Topeka, Kansas, on June 14. *Denver Post* and *Rocky Mountain News* (Denver), June 10–15, 1912.

17. His official death certificate gives 1884 as the birth year, but 1886 appears on his card in the professional baseball contract files maintained annually by *The Sporting News* and 1883 on his membership card in the Association of Professional Ball Players of America. Obituaries stated that he died at age sixty-six, which would support 1884 as the correct birth year. The respective documents are located in the Tennessee Department of Health, Nashville; the membership files of the APBPA in Garden Grove, California; and TSN Archives. All published references and his official death certificate cite "Harry" as his given name, but newspapers in the Southern Association cities initially referred to him as "Henry" Johnson. See, for example, the *Atlanta Constitution, Georgian* and *Journal,* all for June 17, 1919.

18. *Phoenix Gazette,* March 25, 1933.

19. Based on chronological information provided by Danforth in *Standing the Gaff* (p. 12), Johnson would have married in 1915, the year after his dismissal from the National League. More likely, he married in 1918. Johnson had lived in Chicago from 1912 to 1917, but in 1918 moved to Ionia, Michigan, his wife's hometown. The acceptance of two jobs after the 1918 season that would have meant leaving umpiring also suggests a recent acceptance of familial responsibilities. That Johnson mentions his wife only when discussing his initial meeting with Judge Martin in 1919 also points to a recent marriage.

20. *Blue Book* (St. Petersburg, Fla.: Baseball Blue Book, Inc., 1918–25).

21. I have been unable to determine the circumstances of the adoption. The boy's age was given as six when Johnson was honored in New Orleans in 1949, but ten at the time of his death in 1951. *New Orleans Times-Picayune,* July 27, 1949; *Memphis Press-Scimitar,* February 21, 1951.

22. Interview with Helen Wax, Memphis, Tennessee, September 2, 1993. Her husband, Rabbi James A. Wax, conducted funeral services for Johnson. *Memphis Press-Scimitar,* February 21, 1951, and the Memphis *Commercial Appeal,* February 22, 1951.

23. *Memphis Press-Scimitar,* February 21, 1951.

24. The "rhubarb" dates from early days of professional baseball, when club and league officials encouraged angry confrontations with umpires as a way of entertaining fans. While a concerted effort was made to eliminate drinking, gambling and other "unsavory" aspects of the game, umpire-baiting continued and the arbiters became cultural "folk villains." See "America's Manufactured Villain—the Baseball Umpire," in David Q. Voigt, *America*

through Baseball (Chicago: Nelson-Hall, 1976), pp. 162–80.

25. *Louisville Journal* and *Louisville Courier-Journal,* December 4–6, 1922; and *The Sporting News,* December 14, 1922. Judge Martin was also scheduled to address the group, and it is probably through his influence that Johnson was invited to offer remarks.

26. *Phoenix Gazette,* March 25, 1933.

27. The APBPA was founded on October 9, 1924, not 1933 as Johnson states. According to Chuck Stevens, former major league player and long-time secretary-treasurer, the Association currently has a membership of some 13,000, and has serviced 59,000 persons since its founding. Unlike the more recent and highly publicized Baseball Assistance Team (BATS), the APBPA provides assistance to minor leaguers and maintains a low profile in order to avoid calling attention to personal difficulties. Personal interview with Stevens, August 5, 1993.

28. I have not been able to determine which APBPA benefit game Johnson worked. It may have been 1933, the date he cites for the founding of the organization. That spring he accompanied the New York Giants to Los Angeles for a series of exhibition games, and likely confused the year of the benefit game with the founding of the APBPA. See the *Arizona Republic* (Phoenix) and *Phoenix Gazette,* March 25–26, 1933. According to Richard Beverage, the preeminent authority on Los Angeles–area professional baseball, numerous postseason "all-star" and "barnstorming" games were held in the 1920s and 1930s to benefit the APBPA. Chuck Stevens recalled strong support from movie stars like Douglas Fairbanks, Sr., and Tom Mix, who played in "all-star" games with proceeds going to the organization. Personal interviews with Beverage, August 4, 1993, and Stevens, August 5, 1993.

29. For an overview of minor league baseball, see Robert Obojski, *Bush League: A History of Minor League Baseball* (New York: Macmillan, 1975). See also Robert L. Finch, et al., eds., *The Story of Minor League Baseball* (Columbus, Ohio: The National Association of Professional Baseball Leagues, 1952), and Lloyd Johnson and Miles Wolff, eds., *The Minor League Baseball Encyclopedia* (Durham, N.C.: Baseball America, 1993).

30. Although American League President Byron "Ban" Johnson was well-known for his strong support of umpires and opposition to player rowdyism, Johnson probably wrote to the National because of the influence of Cusak and Mullin, both of whom umpired in that circuit in 1909. Mullin also worked the American League, 1911–12, but likely was angry after being released.

31. *New York Times,* February 11 and April 13, 1914. On the relationship between Hart and Tener, see the *Cleveland Leader,* March 22, 1914; I am indebted to Fred Schuld for this reference.

32. *New York Times,* July 18, 1914; *Sporting Life,* July 17 and 25, August 22, 1914.

33. *New York Times,* July 31 and August 1–4, 1914.

34. *The Sporting Life,* August 15 and 22, 1914.

35. *Cincinnati Enquirer,* September 22 and October 2–7, 1914.

36. Although appointed by the American and National Leagues, the umpires worked the city series under the auspices of the National Commission. L. C. Davis of the *St. Louis Post-Dispatch* commented on October 7 after the first game that "Umps Johnson and O'Brien look like they had traded mugs," and Johnson would "never be mistaken for the advance agent of Madame Yale."

37. *Sporting Life,* February 6, 1915. Hart was released after the 1915 season, as were first-year men George Cockill and J. M. Stockdale.

38. *Sporting Life,* August 22, 1914.

39. *Spalding's Official Base Ball Guide . . . for 1915* (Chicago: A. G. Spalding & Bros., 1915), pp. 7–8.

40. *Rocky Mountain News* (Denver), June 10, 1912.

41. *Dubuque Times-Journal,* September 4, 1913.

42. *Standing the Gaff,* p. 38. Cockill was not without important connections. A career minor league player, Cockill led Reading of the Tri-State League in hits (144) and home runs (12) in 1911. In 1912 he took over the Harrisburg club, and led the team to pennants in 1912 and 1914 and second place in 1913. Cockill may have been a good manager, but was less successful as an umpire and released after single season.

43. All professional baseball leagues adopted an abbreviated schedule for 1918, setting a 140-game slate instead of the normal 154. Not even the majors completed the schedule, as the owners ended the season on Labor Day.

44. The official name of the circuit was the Southern Association. Technically, there was no Southern League until 1964, when the South Atlantic League, elevated the year before to Class AA status, changed its name. (The Southern Association disbanded for economic reasons after 1961 season.)

45. Originally designated a Class B circuit, the Southern was upgraded to Class A in 1905. In 1936 the Southern Association and the Texas League were accorded A1 status, and then ten years later were promoted to AA with the creation of the AAA classification for the top three minor league circuits.

46. Norman Elberfeld played shortstop for fourteen years in the majors, ending his career with the Dodgers the year Steamboat reached the National League. He earned the nickname The Tobasco Kid because of his fiery temper. Player-manager of the last-place New York Highlanders in 1908, Elberfeld was known as a contentious hot-head throughout his managerial career in the minors.

47. *Arkansas Democrat* (Little Rock) and *Arkansas Gazette* (Little Rock), April 24–May 6, 1919. Johnson's account that he tossed Elberfeld before the first game of the season is not correct; he did, however, have a sharp exchange with Elberfeld before the first contest and thus likely melded that incident with the subsequent ejections. See W. N. Stone, *Arkansas Democrat,* May 1.

48. Atlanta *Georgian, Atlanta Constitution,* and *Atlanta Journal,* June 17, 1919.

49. *Atlanta Journal,* June 23.

50. The Danforth explanation is plausible, but seems at odds with Johnson's known conduct. It is true, however, as Memphis sportswriter George Lapidis recalled: "You didn't argue with him a lot." Lapidis interview, September 2, 1993. An article in the *Phoenix Gazette,* March 25, 1933, links the nickname "Bulldog" to his tearing open boxes with his teeth. The same explanation was repeated in *The Sporting News,* October 28, 1943 and February 28, 1951. In the *Nashville Tennessean,* July 7, 1943, sports editor Raymond Johnson mentioned that Johnson was once called "Bulldog" and that "his pugilistic tendencies have mellowed with age." Danforth, in his obituary on Johnson, mentions the previous nickname without explanation. *Atlanta Journal,* February 22, 1951.

51. Atlanta *Georgian* and *Atlanta Journal,* June 17, 1919. For reasons unknown, Danforth did not reveal in either the foreword or in Johnson's obituary that he was the sportswriter who coined the "Steamboat" moniker. *Atlanta Journal,* February 22, 1951.

52. Orville Henry, *Arkansas Gazette* (Little Rock), February 22, 1951.

53. *Chattanooga News-Free Press* and *Atlanta Journal,* June 14, 1919; Charlie Hurth, ed., *Southern Association Baseball Records from 1901 to 1947* (New Orleans, Southern Association, 1947), p. 47–48.

54. Hurth, *Southern Association Records,* p. 9.

55. Quoted in Bob Deindorfer, "Steamboat Steals the Show," p. 15, unidentified magazine article in *TSN* Archives.

56. Ibid.

57. *Nashville Banner,* February 21, 1951.

58. Walter Stewart, Memphis *Commercial Appeal,* July 27, 1949; Fred Russell, *Nashville Banner,* February 21, 1951.

59. Memphis *Commercial Appeal,* February 22, 1951.

60. The story was frequently repeated in print. See, for example, the *Nashville Tennessean,* July 8, 1943, and the Memphis *Commercial Appeal,* February 22, 1951, as well as the version told by former American League umpire Tommy Connolly, *The Sporting News,* April 16, 1951. Fans, too, told the story. See the accounts of the incident related in a letter to *The Sporting News* by G. J. Flournoy of Mobile, April 23, 1951, and in an unpublished feature

story by Emmett Maum of Memphis, both sent to *The Sporting News*. *TSN* Archives. Thanks to Steven P. Gietschier, Director of Historical Records, for these references.

61. *Nashville Tennessean*, July 7, 1943, and Memphis *Commercial Appeal*, July 27, 1949. Details of Johnson's telling render both versions apocryphal. Oklahoma City had no team in the Western League in 1912; it joined the circuit in 1918. The Denver episode supposedly occurred on the Fourth of July, but the team was out of town from June 30 to July 23.

62. *Nashville Banner*, February 21, 1951.

63. *Memphis Press-Scimitar*, February 21, 1951.

64. William McG. Keefe, *New Orleans Times-Picayune*, October 28, 1949.

65. Will Carruthers, *Memphis Press-Scimitar*, February 21, 1951.

66. Orville Henry, *Arkansas Gazette* (Little Rock), February 22, 1951; Walter Stewart, Memphis *Commercial Appeal*, July 27, 1949.

67. E. T. Bales, *Chattanooga News-Free Press*, February 21, 1951.

68. Quoted in Deindorfer, "Steamboat Steals the Show," p. 15.

69. Memphis *Commercial Appeal*, February 21, 1951; *The Sporting News*, February 28, 1951.

70. Memphis *Commercial Appeal*, February 22, 1951.

71. Orville Henry, *Arkansas Gazette* (Little Rock), February 22, 1951.

72. *Phoenix Gazette*, March 25, 1933.

73. Reportedly an "overflow" crowd, "conservatively estimated at five thousand," left the park "in outraged disappointment" at the "bitter ruination of a perfectly good afternoon's pleasure." The president of the Augusta club offered to refund the cost of the tickets. *Augusta Chronicle*, April 7–8, 1923.

74. Ed Danforth, *Atlanta Journal*, February 22, 1951.

75. At various points in history, some umpires have been suspected of being "on the take," and in 1884 Dick Higham was expelled from the National League for advising gamblers how to bet on games he umpired. See Larry R. Gerlach, "Richard Higham," in Fred Ivor-Campbell, ed., *Nineteenth-Century Stars* (Cleveland: Society for American Baseball Research, forthcoming 1994).

76. The numerous reprintings and retellings of the story agree in all essentials. See, for example, the *Atlanta Journal*, August 5, 1943, and the *Detroit Free Press*, February 21, 1951.

77. *The Sporting News*, October 28, 1943.

78. Players from each of the forty-one minor leagues were divided into teams named the Doubledays and the Cartwrights; the former won the contest 9–6. The other umpires were also distinguished veterans: Charley

Moore of the Eastern League (A) at first base, ex-major leaguer Ollie Anderson of the Western Association (C) at second, and former major leaguer Bill Carpenter of the International League (AA) at third. *The Sporting News*, July 10, 1939. See also the *New York Times*, July 10, 1939.

79. *Nashville Banner*, July 9–10, and *Nashville Tennessean*, July 7–10, 1943. Actually, he received an empty box, as the time piece had not arrived from Atlanta where it was being engraved; the Steamer did not actually receive the watch until he returned to Atlanta's Ponce de Leon Park. Newspaper reports and the inscription are incorrect, as the ceremony marked his twenty-fourth year in the Southern. It would have been a quarter-century had he not worked in the South Atlantic in 1921.

80. Danforth, *Atlanta Journal*, August 5, 1943. Reprinted as "Valiant Is the Word for 'Steamboat,'" in *Baseball Digest* 2 (September 1943), p. 57–58. See also an undated *New York Daily News* article, *TSN* Archives. Jones noted that "Steamer had written those words down and read 'em off to me. By now he has them memorized. If you meet him, he'll show you the watch and tell you just what valiant means." The honor did not leave the Steamer awash in sentimentality. It gave him a new quip: Whenever he was asked the time of day, he concluded his response by saying "and, like my umpiring, that is the correct time."

81. Memphis *Commercial Appeal*, December 4–5, 1946.

82. *Nashville Tennessean*, February 23, 1951; *Arkansas Gazette* (Little Rock), February 21, 1951.

83. *New Orleans Times-Picayune*, July 24–29, 1949; Memphis *Commercial Appeal*, July 26–27, 1949. See also James M. Kahn, *The Umpire Story* (New York: G. P. Putnam's Sons, 1953), pp. 197–98.

84. Lou Jorda, after six years in the Southern Association, was promoted to the National League in 1927 only to be sent down to the International League (AA) in 1932; he was recalled in 1940 and remained to the Senior Circuit until retiring in 1952. Buck Campbell, a Memphis native and close friend of Johnson's, worked five years in the Southern before going to the American League in 1928; he returned to Southern in 1932 and after seven seasons was hired by the National League in 1939.

85. *Nashville Banner*, March 16, 1951.

86. Lapidis interview, September 2, 1993.

87. Memphis *Commercial Appeal*, February 22, 1951.

88. George Bugbee, *Memphis Press-Scimitar*, February 21, 1951.

Advertising Section

Semi-Norfolk Back
GoldSmith
UMPIRES' UNIFORMS
Tailored to individual measurements
From all-wool, twelve-ounce serge
Special folder with actual samples of materials and full descriptions and prices is yours for the asking.
THE P. GoldSmith SONS, Inc.
CINCINNATI, OHIO, U. S. A.

GoldSmith

OFFICIAL LEAGUE BALL

No. 97

The Official Baseball of The Southern Association

No. 276

No. CUB

GoldSmith

UMPIRES' EQUIPMENT

Used and endorsed by leading umpires in Major and Minor Leagues

No. CFP

Umpires' Masks
Umpires' Shoes
Body Protectors
Leg Guards
Supporters
Indicators

No. CUW

Write for descriptive folder

No. CUL

THE P. GoldSmith SONS, Inc.

CINCINNATI, OHIO, U. S. A.

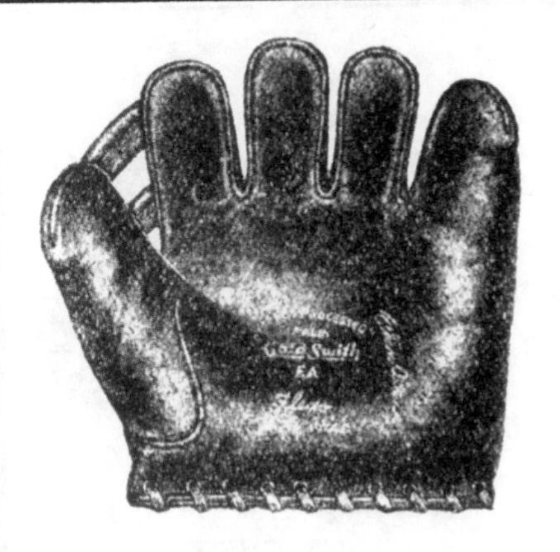

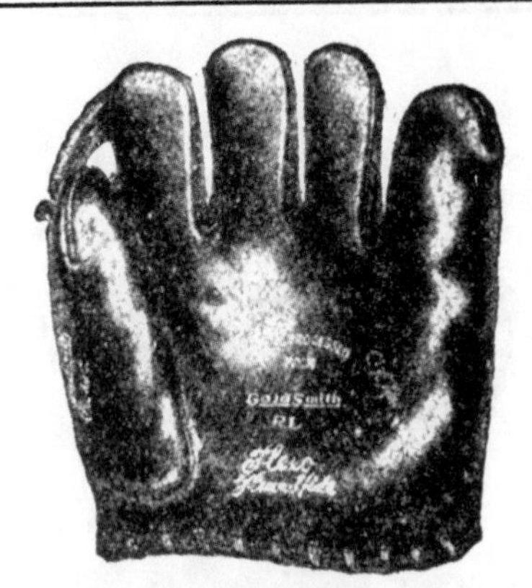

GoldSmith

Professional Model

Fielders' Gloves

Basemen's Mitts

Catchers' Mitts

A complete line of autographed gloves and mitts used by leading National and American League players.

Catalogue with full descriptions and prices gladly sent upon request.

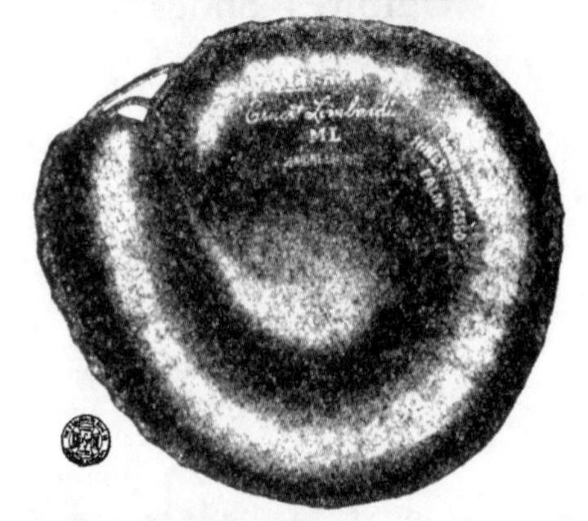

THE P. GoldSmith SONS, Inc.

CINCINNATI, OHIO, U. S. A.

GoldSmith

Professional League Baseball Uniforms as Supplied to Major and Minor Leagues

1. Double-shrunk virgin wool flannel
2. Triple-stitched seams
3. Ventilated crotch and armpits
4. Tailored to individual measure. Plenty of roominess
5. Choice of heavy leather or elastic belt
6. Pure worsted ribbed hose made any color or style, with feet or footless
7. Fully trimmed and lettered in any style and color

Send for folder giving full descriptions and prices

THE P. GoldSmith SONS, Inc.

CINCINNATI, OHIO, U. S. A.

Umpires Have Parents

A Few Words on the Origin and Upbringing of the Man Who Was to Become a Colorful Member of a Lonely Guild

A FOREWORD

By Ed Danforth

THIS is "Steamboat" Johnson's book. No literary ghost wrote it for him. "Steamboat" wrote it out in longhand in his off hours during the 1935 season. An umpire actually has lots of time available for literary effort. Of his job it has been said, "You can't beat them hours." It is a wonder so few of them ever have taken time to jot down the stirring events of which they have been the center. Their view of the melodramatic spectacle that is baseball is far different from that of the fan in the bleachers, the player on the field or the sports writers in the press box.

It was something like five years ago that I asked "Steamboat" to let me write his life history. I suggested that he knew a lot about baseball that never had been told, a lot that is seen only through the mask of the man in blue. "Steamboat" promised he would do it. Then I forgot all about it.

One day in the late summer of 1935, "Steamboat" called me and said HE was writing the story of his life. What is more he had taken steps toward printing and publishing it. He was characteristically forceful and direct about it all. He was moving with a speed no literary gentleman ever could achieve.

The manuscript was delivered to me in a huge bundle a few weeks ago with the request that I edit it and arrange it for publication. That chore proved interesting in more ways than one. I discovered that "Steamboat" had told no end of delightful tales of the diamond, but had omitted what may be the most interesting part. He had neglected to tell a thing about himself and his origin and his background. Few realize that after all umpires have parents and brothers and sisters, go to school, and grow up as normal boys. I had to corner "Steamboat" and worm a lot of that information out of him. It may never have been published before.

* * *

ONE March morning word went through the town of Pottsville, Pa., in the heart of the anthracite region, that Sam and Rosalie Johnson had another baby at their house. It was the sixth—three brothers and two sisters were waiting for him. The youngest of the Johnsons was named Harry

Samuel. The miners dropped in at Big Sam's saloon to shake hands and exchange broad jokes about the blessed event and lift a foaming stein to the new arrival.

Harry grew up to hear tales of the famous Molly Maguires, a gang of rowdies who had terrorized the town of Pottsville before Harry was born. He had heard his father tell about the rioting many a time. And even in Harry's boyhood, Pottsville was no elegant town in which to live.

The Johnsons moved to the more sedate environs of Elmira, N. Y., just after Harry reached school age and there he grew up. Sam Johnson was highly respected and his place downtown was always clean and orderly. Little Harry often tended bar while his father was at home for dinner and early learned to have a quick answer for the trade. Yet he never so much as touched a glass of beer and has not to this good day. He never even took a cigar as was the traditional custom of bartenders.

Elmira was the home of "Red" Murray, Giant outfielder; Joe Birmingham, the hard-hitting Cleveland Indian; Frank (Fielder) Jones, manager of the White Sox; and Danny Richardson, second baseman for the Giants. No wonder, then, that this offshoot of good Irish-German stock should have drifted into sandlot baseball and played on his grade school team.

Harry was a left-handed first baseman and a good one. He tried out for the football team and wanted to play quarterback but the coach insisted on playing him at fullback.

"I soon found I was getting nothing but black eyes and cracked shins out of it and was not allowed to hit back, so I quit the squad," Johnson says now. There may be some sound philosophy in that.

* * *

HARRY'S pugnacious disposition and his willingness to engage in a fight on the slightest provocation earned him the nickname of "Bulldog" which persisted until 1919, when the title of "Steamboat" was conferred on him and caught the public fancy.

Harry graduated from grade school in a classification that now would be rated junior high and the family moved to Wilkinsburg, a suburb of Pittsburgh, Pa., where a better business opportunity opened for the elder Johnson. There Harry organized a semi-pro team for which he was first baseman and manager. They were called the "Crab Hollers" by the fans. The origin of the name is shrouded in mystery. It was while managing this team that Harry decided to become an umpire.

Twenty-one years ago, Harry was working in a Chicago department store in the off season. Jimmy

Hamilton, now president of the Nashville ball club, also was employed there. Jimmy introduced Harry to Miss Bertha Miller, who was down from her home in Ionia, Mich., visiting friends. A year later Harry and Bertha were married. He promised her faithfully he would give up baseball. That was the only promise he never kept and, I suspect, never intends to keep.

They are still happily married. They live in Memphis, where he operates "Steamboat Johnson's Eat Shoppe," a favorite restaurant for cotton men. Mrs. Johnson attends all games in Memphis when "Steamboat" is working, but she is the perfect neutral and never roots for either team.

* * *

STEAMBOAT JOHNSON is as full of color as a circus parade. He is one umpire who is a standout even on the always capable staff of umpires in the Southern League. He is a real gate attraction. Fans often come to the park just to see him work.

"Steamboat" is aggressive, dynamic, forceful. He is absolutely impartial. He knows the rules inside and out. Ball players and managers are neither friends nor enemies. They are impersonal units in a contest, the direction of which he has in his hands. His is the true judicial mentality.

So why shouldn't "Steamboat" Johnson write his own book, his life story? Every man is entitled to tell about his life as he sees it. It stands, too, as the saga of an umpire that may reveal the strange world in which the members of that profession move. From April to October they have little human association save with their partners. They mingle neither with ball players nor with the public. I think "The Steamer" has given us in this book a glimpse of his essentially lonely craft.

ED DANFORTH,
Sports Editor, Atlanta Georgian.

DECEMBER 1, 1935.

The First Game—The First Row

HARRY JOHNSON TALKS HIMSELF INTO BECOMING AN UMPIRE—CALLS FORMER TEAMMATE OUT AT HOME AND IS ABUSED—HIS FIRST PROFESSIONAL CONTRACT SIGNED

IT was in 1909 that I talked myself into becoming a baseball umpire. I was manager and part owner of a baseball club in a little town in Pennsylvania just outside Pittsburgh that year, and the fans did not like the man I had engaged to umpire our games. They kept after me to get a different umpire for every game, for what reason I do not know. If I answered the question once I answered it a hundred times. I always said: "This man I have engaged is a good umpire. He is always hustling and he runs the game like I would run it if I was an umpire."

By the end of our regular playing season that idea had taken hold of me. I knew how a game should be run by an umpire and I decided to try my hand at it. I started working in late games played outside Pittsburgh and kept working until it became too cold for even those hardy Pennsylvanians to play.

I ran into trouble in my very first game, over 25

years ago, and I have been running into it ever since.

My first jam was like this:

Several of the players who had worked for me during the summer were picking up a little extra change playing for one of these late season teams. I was getting along all right but in the ninth inning a close play came up at home plate and I called it against the runner who had been the field captain of my team during the summer. I called him out with the tying run. He bounced up out of the dirt and shouted:

"A swell friend of mine you are. I never would have expected you to call one like that on me."

I replied:

"Friend or no friend, you were out and you still are out."

That man has never spoken to me to this good day. The decision was discussed all winter and while some of them put me in the grease, most of them said I had nerve.

That experience and all the talk that winter convinced me that I had what it took to stand the gaff, and, with encouragement from some of my friends, I decided to go after regular games the next season.

* * *

It was in 1910 that I met Richard Guy, who then was sporting editor of the Pittsburgh *Gazette*. He saw me work and told me I could make good in professional baseball. Guy recommended me to George Moreland, president of the old Ohio and Pennsylvania League, and it paved the way for me to break in.

The Pittsburgh district was full of baseball teams in those days and many who later became famous in the major leagues were on the sandlots and semi-pro teams learning the game.

From this section came such players as Hans Lobert, Otto Knabe, Lew Moren, Charlie Deal, Bill McKechnie, Al Mamaux, Cliff Markle, Billy Bayne, and others that I was to meet later in leagues all over the country. It was a baseball center and no mistake about it.

* * *

During the winter of 1910-11, I signed my first contract and opened the season at Youngstown with Lee Fohl's Akron team as the visiting club. Two of the Youngstown players were Bert Shotten and Everett Scott. That seems a long way to most fans, I guess, and it does to me, too.

I was working the games alone in those days. I had to stand behind the plate and call plays at second base which between us was guessing, but I got by all right. The players were used to working with one umpire and they got the idea early that I was calling them as I saw them. I had trouble but I did not lose courage. It was a strain trying to call plays correctly when I was not in position to see them properly.

That winter I began putting out my lines to get a job in a league that used the double system of umpiring. I ran across a man named John Mullen, who later on umpired in the Southern League and had had major league experience. We had long talks and he gave me a lot of advice. He wrote a letter to Tip O'Neill, president of the Western League, giving me a big boost.

That was the word that gave me a break. It was just a few days after I wrote to President O'Neill applying for the job that I received a contract from him which I signed immediately.

Where Men Meant Business

JACK O'TOOLE BATTLES CLUB OWNER—"STEAMBOAT" HAS FIRST AND LAST EXPERIENCE WITH ATTEMPT TO "FIX" A GAME—WITH PISTOLS, TOO

I OPENED the season of 1912 in the Western League paired with a man named Myers, working with him half the season. Double-teaming was a mile ahead of the old single umpire system and I soon learned to call plays right on bases. In the middle of the season I was switched to work with Jack O'Toole, who later was to umpire in the Southern League. Then things began to happen.

I'll never forget the fight O'Toole had with Jack Holland, owner of the St. Joe club, right in the St. Joe umpires' dressing room. Neither will Jack Holland. It was a row over a decision O'Toole had called against the home club, one word leading to trouble, as so often happens when men get excited. The upshot of it was that O'Toole was arrested on complaint of the club owner and hauled off to police station. I went down and posted the amount of the bond. When the matter was brought to the attention of President O'Neill, he took steps and had the case postponed. Later it was dropped and my bond money was returned to me intact.

* * *

The race that year was close and during the last week of the season Jack and I were assigned to Denver to handle the critical series between Denver and Omaha. Jack Hendricks was managing Denver then and Bill Abrogast was managing Omaha.

It was there that I was approached for the first and last time by parties who wanted to influence my decisions. Jack and I arrived in Denver and went to the Hotel St. James. We were assigned to our room and after we had unpacked we went downstairs to the lobby. We took seats in chairs and pretty soon two men came up. They moved close to us and, opening their coats, showed us the butts of pistols tucked in their belts. They did not waste any words. They said:

"Do you two fellows see these"—indicating the pistols—"Well, we have a lot of lead for you if you do not call every close decision in favor of Denver. We'll be at the game watching you."

Jack and I both stood up and Jack said:

"The guns don't mean a thing to us. This is no wild west show. Get out of this hotel lobby before we start something."

They said nothing, turned around and left. We thought no more about it except to wonder if it was a practical joke someone had played on us. Early the next morning, however, our telephone rang. Jack answered it and it was one of the gunmen. He warned us he would be at the game that day with his gang and pistols ready, watching us. He hung up before Jack could say anything.

It so happened that Denver beat Omaha by a big score and close decisions did not affect the course of the game. Sometimes I wonder what might have happened if we had had to call an Omaha player safe at home with the winning run in the ninth inning.

From that day to this, I have never been approached by any man in regard to throwing a ball game his way. It speaks well for the profession, I think, that gamblers do not even consider attempting to bribe or intimidate an umpire. They have gone to ball players, but they always leave umpires alone.

* * *

It was during that season of 1912 that I got into trouble over a ground rule. I may say here that ground rules have sent more umpires back to their hotels with pop bottle bumps on the skull than any other one feature of baseball.

Omaha was playing in Des Moines one Sunday afternoon and eight or nine thousand people were out. We had a rule that a man on third could score if a ball pitched from the rubber hit the backstop. It was in the eleventh inning and Bert Niehoff, then a young fellow playing third for Omaha, was on third base with the winning run. Well, a pitched ball hit the backstop, and I immediately waved Bert home.

The stands let out a yell, and Frank Isbell, Des Moines manager, came running up and protested, claiming the ball did not hit the stand. I told him that I had seen it and that Niehoff's run counted.

With that Isbell grabbed my protector and jerked it off, the straps snapping with the force of his effort. Then I saw several Des Moines players coming on the run, so I grabbed Isbell and threw him to the ground. In a moment all the Des Moines players were on me pulling and hauling, but unable to get at me very well because I was tied up with Isbell. I ordered all of them back to their positions and warned I would forfeit the game if they did not obey. Isbell ordered them back, too, and we resumed play. I was without a protector, as the straps were broken.

Des Moines came to bat, but went out one-two-three, and the game was over with Niehoff's run winning it.

As the last man went out at first base, the crowd

poured out of the grandstand and surrounded me, pushing and yelling. They started swinging, and I went down with a couple of rights to the ear; but I scrambled up and got into the grandstand, where several policemen gave me protection and helped me get to my dressing room. It was an hour before the crowd left and I could get to a street car.

Every time I worked in Des Moines after that I was razzed from start to finish.

The Old "101 Ranch"

Western League Was Rough on Umpires—"Steamboat" Sees Brother Killed by Bandit—"Manicure Act" Balks Fans in Riot

THE old Western League was a honey. It was the toughest of all in those days. The umpires called it the "101 Ranch." It was a Wild West show from the start, one riot after another, and a stream of players always leaving the field.

I do not know how many players were put out that year, but I do know that at the end of the season they released every one of us umpires, saying we were too hard on the players. For our part, I can say that the players and the fans certainly were rough on the umpires. I must say also that President O'Neill was a real man and backed up every one of us while the season was in progress.

The season of 1912 stands out in my memory for another incident that did not happen on the baseball field. I had a brother in Denver who operated a drug store at Seventeenth and Broadway. I had not seen him in fourteen years until I came in to umpire a series there.

On the evening of July 10, which was a Sunday, I was in his store drinking a soda that he had just made for me. He had walked to the other side of the store and was behind the counter. As I lifted my glass, I felt something poked into the small of my back and heard a man's voice say: "Hands up, you!"

I thought it a joke by one of my brother's friends or maybe a ball player, so I turned around laughing. But I saw it was no joke. The man had a handkerchief tied across his eyes with holes to see through and, what is more, he had a blue-steel gun that was pointed at my stomach. I put up my hands, and he told me to to walk back to the rear of the store. Then he caught sight of my brother coming out from behind the counter. He pointed the gun at him and ordered him to follow me to the rear.

My brother did so, but as he passed along by a low counter he reached over it for a pistol he kept underneath. The bandit rushed to him, poked the pistol into my brother's side and fired.

A woman who had walked into the store with a prescription saw the whole tragedy from her place near the soda counter. She saw the bandit keep me covered while he opened the cash register and took out all the money he could find and then saw him run from the store. I took out after him, but he got away.

Meanwhile, my brother had walked over to a divan that was kept there for customers to use while waiting for prescriptions to be filled, and had collapsed on it. I called a hospital and soon the ambulance had taken him away. He died the next day.

Fortunately the woman testified at the inquest that she had seen the shooting, or it would have been up to me to prove I did not do it.

I have been looking for that bandit ever since.

I will never forget how his chin looked and how his ears were set on his head.

That was all of his features I could see on account of the handkerchief he wore as a mask, but it is enough for me to identify him.

I keep looking at the faces I see in the baseball crowds—yes, and even on the baseball field—and one of these days I will see that chin and those ears that I saw in the drug store in Denver so long ago.

* * *

In the winter of 1912-13 I went to Chicago to spend a few days, and there I met an umpire by the name of Steve Cusack, who I later was to learn was one of the finest men I ever knew and a credit to the profession.

Steve was working in the Three-Eye League and also connected with the Boston Department Store.

Steve got me a position there for the winter, and I made good from the start. It was to provide me with winter employment for several years.

Several ball players and umpires worked there, and we called it our "winter home." Among the umpires were Frank McNulty, Western League; George Johnson, American Association; Guy Colgate, Virginia League; Cusack, and I.

The ball players employed were Jimmy Hamilton, then in the Three-Eye League, and Fred Gilmore of the American Association.

Superintendent R. G. Mangold liked all of us and the way we worked, and I believe any of us could go back there and get a job now if we needed one.

* * *

Steve asked me to work with him in the Three-Eye League the season of 1913, and so I applied in person to Al Tierney, president, whose office was in Chicago at the time. On Steve's recommendation, President Tierney gave me a contract, and there began a connection that I never regretted. President Tierney was one of the finest league presidents I ever worked for. He always backed up his umpires even when club owners took issue with us.

I will never forget some of the jams we got into that year, especially one at Davenport, Iowa, when

Danville, Ill., was the visiting club. I was working alone that day. I had begun carrying a six-inch snap-blade knife in my hip pocket during the stormy days in the Western League, and I had it on me then.

Two men were out in the ninth when a Davenport outfielder hit a three-bagger down the left field line. In rounding first base he missed the bag, but I never gave any indication that I had seen it.

When the ball was relayed to the infield, the Danville first baseman called for the ball and touched the bag. I immediately called the runner out, which ended the game, Danville winning.

As I started for the dressing room the crowd began tumbling over the front of the grandstand and moving toward me. I reached into my hip pocket, pulled out my knife, snapped the blade open, and began cutting my finger nails. I pretended to be paying no attention to them. They stopped, and took it out in calling me names. Then I started walking along, trimming my nails as I went. I walked to the gate and out to the street car, still wearing my protector and carrying my mask under one arm, and was not molested. I never had any more trouble in Davenport that season.

It was the last week of the season that I ran into another jam that left me something to remember Dubuque by.

Quincy, Ill., was playing there. Clarence (Pants) Rowland was the Dubuque manager and Nick Kahl was the Quincy manager. The two teams were fighting tooth and nail for the pennant, and Quincy needed two out of three games to win.

They might have figured this one out in the movies, but it happened to me in real life: in the last game of the season I had to call the tying run out at the plate, and the game was over with Quincy winning the pennant on my decision.

Well, the crowd rushed out on the field after me. I was working with a man named Bannon, and he was right at my shoulder as soon as he saw the crowd coming. The mob started hitting at me, but there were so many of them they got in each other's way. I managed to keep my feet and reached the dressing room safely.

The crowd charged up to the door. I picked up a chair and handed my snap blade knife to Bannon.

The Irishman went over the top swinging the knife in front of him and the crowd took it on the lam. It was a close call. We had to stay in our room for an hour. Finally we got away, and when we reached our hotel, they were waiting for us in the lobby. The manager of the hotel ran them out somehow and we got safely inside, tired out from our excitement.

One day in Peoria I chased Barry McCormick, the manager, and it brought the crowd after me, yelling and cursing. I had chased Barry, so they chased me. I hid in a shed in which were stored the tools, lime, grass seed, and such that were used to keep the field in shape. Police rescued me and saw me safely on the street car. Later on, McCormick became an umpire, and I wonder if he ever remembered the day he was on the other side of the argument.

McGraw Sent to Showers

"STEAMBOAT" WORKED IN NATIONAL LEAGUE IN 1914—RULED "RED" MURRAY CAUGHT FLY IN THUNDERSTORM—HANDLED ST. LOUIS CITY SERIES—RELEASED—WHY?

MANY fans have asked whether I ever umpired in the major leagues or not and why I did not spend most of my career in the big show instead of in the minors.

It was in the fall of 1913 that I wrote to President Tom Lynch of the National League asking for a chance. That was my first contact with one of the finest men baseball has ever claimed. He was an able executive, and in his dealings with umpires he was the sort of man the boys in blue dream of having in the head office. He told his umpires to run that ball game and assured them that he was behind them from start to finish.

In a short time, a letter came from John Heydler, who was secretary of the league at that time, asking for my terms and assuring me that my recommendations were entirely satisfactory. I wired back:

"Your terms are my terms. I will be perfectly

satisfied for the chance to work in the National League."

I was working in Chicago at the time for the Boston Store, and within a week my contract came for an amount that pleased me greatly. I said nothing about it and worked on through the winter. In the spring of 1914 I was ordered to report in New York for a meeting with the new president, John K. Tener, who had been elected to succeed Tom Lynch.

All during the winter I had been wondering who my working partner would be, and I had hoped it would be Bill Klem, who I thought was one of the greatest umpires who ever wore the blue. I called on the secretary, and he told me that I had been highly spoken of by everyone who knew me and that I would have no trouble making good.

After the conference, I was notified that I would be an extra umpire and was instructed to hold myself in readiness to report anywhere. When the Eastern clubs were in the West, I would be stationed at either Cincinnati or Pittsburgh; and when the Western clubs were in the East, I would be based in New York.

I was very much disappointed not to become a regular man due to the wide experience I had had, but I determined to make the best of it. I worked a few games during the early part of the season.

Finally Al Orth, a fine umpire and a prince of a fellow, hurt his knee in Philadelphia, and I received orders to join Bill Byron. I no time I discovered that Bill was a great one to work with, and we got along famously through about eighty games.

* * *

My worst jam was in New York one day when John McGraw was managing the Giants and Charlie Herzog had his Cincinnati Reds in town. About 40,000 people were in the Polo Grounds that day, and I was working the bases. Big Jeff Tesreau was pitching for the Giants and Larry Benton for the Reds. Something came up and a big argument started with me in the center of it.

Finally I chased Tesreau, McGraw, and Mike Donlin. The three of them took it good-naturedly, and they lock-stepped their way across the field to the clubhouse. That act got me a few bottles all right, but none of them hit me.

Let me say here and now that John McGraw was a great manager and a fine man and one of the outstanding characters in baseball, who rendered the game a great service.

* * *

I worked in what became a famous game in Pittsburgh during that season between the Pirates and the

Giants. It was one of the longest games on record up to that time—twenty-two innings—with Christy Mathewson and Babe Adams in a great pitching duel.

In the twenty-second inning the Giants came to bat and scored a run to take the lead.

The Pirates came up for their half. It had grown dark and rain was threatening. Heavy clouds covered the sky and flashes of lightning broke through every now and then. Soon they had two men on base and two out. The last hitter smacked one to the center field wall, and "Red" Murray, Giant centerfielder, started running toward where he thought the ball would come down.

While the ball was in the air, it started to rain in earnest. A big flash of lightning burst over the field, and the next moment it was all the darker by contrast. I was working the bases that day and Bill Byron was behind the plate. I ran toward the center field wall and got some distance into the outfield, when I saw Murray catch the ball in his gloved hand near the wall. I signaled the batter out and the game was over.

There are old-time fans in Pittsburgh to this day who will tell you that "Red" Murray did not catch that ball, that it was lost in the rain and darkness.

* * *

During that season I was appointed to work the

annual baseball game between the Army and the Navy at Annapolis. I also handled an exhibition game between the Pirates and the White Sox and another one for the Willys-Overland people in Toledo between the Athletics and the Braves. Tom Connolly and I worked that day in Toledo. He is umpire-in-chief of the American League and certainly was one of the top men in the profession.

I finished out the season in Cincinnati with Byron. Just after the game was over while we were getting ready to pack up and go home, Bill received a wire telling him he had been appointed a World's Series umpire, and I had one telling me that I was to work in the city series in St. Louis between the Browns and the Cardinals. You can imagine how happy we both were to get those breaks!

Byron told me that he felt sure I had made good in my first year as a National League umpire and that getting the assignment to work the city series in St. Louis when other umpires were overlooked meant that I was a sure shot for the next season.

On arrival in St. Louis I found Joe O'Brien was there from the American League to work with me. We had a conference with Manager Branch Rickey, of the Browns, and Manager Miller Huggins, of the Cardinals. They told us that the year before the series had ended up in a pop-bottle riot and that they were anxious to avoid anything like that this year. So they both agreed that the umpires were to run the game and that any player or manager put out of the game should leave the field immediately and without argument.

Everything went off smoothly, the Browns finished as city champions, and everybody was well pleased with our work.

Several managers had the kindest sort of things to say about my work that year, including Fred Clarke, of the Pirates; Wilbert Robinson, of the Dodgers; George Stallings, of the Braves; Red Dooin, of the Phillies; Charlie Herzog, of the Reds; Miller Huggins, of the Cardinals; and John McGraw, of the Giants.

Along in December I received a letter from Secretary Heydler saying that the league could not see its way clear to retain me on the staff, but that he knew I would have no trouble in getting a good position in the minors. That nearly floored me. My friends, too, were surprised. I wrote Secretary Heydler asking why I was not retained, and to this day I have never received a reply. In my place an old-time catcher named George Cockrill who had never umpired a game was signed, and that was that.

I decided to work hard and get another chance in the majors, but I never got the break.

Honor Guest Is Chased

PUTS OUT "CHIEF" MYERS ON HIS "DAY" IN BUFFALO—GETS 4-INCH SCAR IN FIGHT AT TROY—N. Y. STATE AND INTERNATIONAL LEAGUE JAMS

I HAD no trouble signing with President John Farrell, of the New York State League. I worked with him in 1915, 1916, and 1917. Mr. Farrell was appointed president of the International League in 1918, and I immediately was signed as umpire in that league.

My three years in the New York State League were exciting. I learned a lot about umpiring in those years. A man can learn something new about his work every day, and I found that I picked up something new and useful in my line every afternoon on the ball field.

One of the toughest afternoons I ever had was in Utica, N. Y.

The game was moving right along, and we were near setting a record for time. The crowd was enjoying the game immensely; but when I called a batter out on a third strike to end the game, they raised sand. They wanted the game to go on, I suppose, and there was nothing in the rules to permit it to do so. They came rushing out on the field, and the police had to see me home as they often did.

That was the only time I ever saw fans object to having a game moved along fast and ended quickly. We always try to keep the teams hustling and take great pride in setting short time records, but for once we were wrong. Maybe they had nowhere else to go and nothing else to do in Utica.

* * *

It was in Troy, N. Y., that I got a four-inch scar over my right eye that I carry to this day.

It all came about in the eleventh inning of a game with Utica. Evans, of the Utica club, was on third base, and he stole home to win the game. I called him safe, which was exactly as I saw it.

The Troy catcher named McGrath started arguing, and several other Troy players joined in. The Troy second baseman made a pass at me. I ducked and let go a swing that landed on the side of his head and knocked him down. Catcher McGrath swung his mask and caught me over the right eye, and I went down.

As I was lying there with the players milling about over me, I found blood was streaming from my cut eye. I put my handkerchief over my eye and held it in place with my cap. Then I sat up and ordered five players out of the game. I scrambled to my feet and ordered the game to go on. I finished the rest of the game with one eye, as the blood was obscuring the sight of the other.

When the game was over, the police came to escort me to the gate. I had to pass under a railroad trestle to get to the street car, and a bunch of fans on top of it threw coal at me. The police left me and chased them away, and I managed to get back to the hotel with no more trouble. I telegraphed details of the trouble to President Farrell, and he fined the players who participated in the fight.

I had to have four stitches taken in the cut, by the way, so it will be a long time before I forget Troy.

* * *

One of the wildest fights I ever had was in Wilkesbarre, where mounted policemen had to get me out of the park. I was beaten up by eight or ten men, and I could not straighten up for several days, but I kept on working and never missed a day. You had to be able to take it in Wilkesbarre.

* * *

During the war year of 1918 I was working in the International League, and, due to an economy move, we were using only one umpire in each game. It was the first time in years that I had worked single.

Working alone in a ball game is something else, and naturally I ran into trouble.

One day Toronto was playing in Rochester and in the eleventh inning a Toronto player was on second base.

As I started to brush the dirt off home plate, he stole third and I called him safe. I did not see the play; therefore I could not call him out. If a base umpire had been working with me, he would have seen the play. It was just one of those hazards that come up when working single. Toronto won the game, and my friends, the police, had to see me all the way to my hotel. The crowd hung around the hotel for two hours waiting for me to appear, but I stayed right where I was, having no business to attend to down the street.

* * *

Another tough time that year was when I umpired the only Sunday game ever played in the State of Maryland. Toronto was playing Baltimore at Pimlico, just outside Baltimore, and I had to chase a player named Pug Griffin who was playing first base for the Orioles and Jack Dunn, the manager. Let me say here that Jack was a fine man off the field, but a very tough one to deal with in a ball game.

After the game I had to duck into the bus with the Toronto players, and the crowd gathered around me and began throwing rocks at me. I had to lie down on the floor of the bus, so the crowd would not see me.

* * *

I was the umpire who chased "Chief" Meyers out of the Buffalo park when fans were giving him a testimonial day. He was the same "Chief" Meyers who later caught Christy Mathewson for the Giants. A big noisy crowd was on hand for "Chief Meyers Day," and they gave him a large silver loving cup. About the seventh inning, something came up and I ordered Meyers to take himself and his loving cup out of the park. I had to have my favorite escort of bluecoats to the hotel again.

* * *

Toward the end of the season they gave each of us another umpire as a partner. One day Jack Dunn's Orioles were playing a double header in Toronto, and a man named O'Brien was working with me. Something happened in the first game, and O'Brien forfeited the game to Toronto.

When time came for the second game, Dunn would not take his team on the field, he said, if O'Brien worked. He demanded that I work the second game alone. I refused to go on without my partner, so Dunn finally gave in. We umpires took an awful razzing from the crowd, because they thought we had delayed the game to get a sandwich or something.

Canadian fans are a great bunch. They are well-behaved and always applaud a good play by the visiting team, and generally are very fair with the umpires.

* * *

Polly McLarry, now of the Southern League staff, caught me off guard one day in Baltimore and got me into trouble.

Polly was playing first base for Binghampton. The game went into the last half of the ninth, and Baltimore had the winning run on second with two out. One of the Orioles hit a three bagger into center field that seemed to have won the game, but he missed first base in making his turn, and I saw it.

McLarry was watching me, and he figured something was up from the way I looked. So when the ball was returned to the infield and as the happy crowd was starting out of the park, Polly called for it and touched first. I promptly called the batter out, which retired the side and sent the game into extra innings.

When the game was over—Binghampton won it—the crowd came out after me, and I had to leave the field, walking between two mounted policemen; even the horses seemed sore at me and kept trying to step on me.

My Debut in Southern

"KID" ELBERFELD GIVES ROYAL WELCOME — IS CHASED BEFORE OPENING GAME STARTS—CHRISTENED "STEAMBOAT" BY ED DANFORTH, ATLANTA GEORGIAN SPORTS EDITOR

AFTER the 1918 season was over I returned to Chicago and worked for the Boston Store again. In November, the manager of the store called me in and asked me whether I would quit baseball if they made me a floor manager in their store. I asked them for a few days to think it over. As a matter of fact, I figured it over for two weeks. The idea of dodging pop bottles and having ball players and the crowds after me from April until October and looking around for the police to take me to my hotel was beginning to get a little tiresome, I thought.

Meanwhile an offer came as branch manager of a chemical concern in Omaha. The upshot of it was that I accepted the offer of the chemical concern and gave up my contract as umpire in the International League.

I had not been in Omaha since 1912 when I was a Western League umpire—in the old "101 Ranch" as the umpires called it—but I found I had many friends there who remembered me. I did very well indeed as branch manager of the store and got a lot of new business.

During the winter, I received several contracts for work, as President Farrell, of the International, had made me a free agent.

It was in March, 1919, that I received a letter from John D. Martin, then the president-elect of the Southern League, saying that he had heard me recommended very highly and that he wanted me to sign a contract with him. He told me some of his ideas of handling his umpires, and they sounded mighty good to me.

As I said, it was March and spring was coming on and I could hear the crowd yelling and the ball hitting in the catcher's glove. I forgot all about the quiet joy of life as a branch manager, and sat down and wrote President Martin that I would like to work for him. I always had wanted to work in the Southern League, and a lot of the managers and players I knew in other leagues were down there. Besides, it seemed warm and pleasant beside the weather we had been having in Omaha.

I notified the company headquarters that I was going back into baseball, and they treated me fairly about it and wished me well. They had another man there to take my place April 1, and I went on to Memphis to report to President Martin.

I shall never forget my first interview with the man with whom I was to be so closely associated for the next few years. He told me what he expected of his umpires and how he expected to handle their reports. I told him:

"There are only two people whose opinions I care anything about. One is you, Mr. Martin. The other is Mrs. Johnson."

President Martin got a kick out of that remark, and he never has forgotten it. The other umpires reported on time, and at our meeting we were assigned to our stations for the opening games.

I was sent to Little Rock, where "Kid" Elberfeld was manager.

* * *

What a welcome I received into the Southern League that day in Little Rock!

When I walked out to home plate to start the game, "Kid" Elberfeld saw I was a new man, so he proceeded to sound me out.

"Well, hello, you car-barn bandit," he shouted. "Where in the world did President Martin get a-hold of you?"

"Right out of a fast league, and if you don't take

it easy you will be riding a street car back to town before the game starts," I said.

"Why, I've heard of you," the "Kid" went on. "You rob street cars in the Chicago barns at night."

"Out you go, 'Kid,' " I said.

"Why, you can't put me out of the game, because it ain't started yet," the "Kid" replied.

"Well, you are out, and I don't see any ball players in the field," I answered.

Well, the "Kid" squawked loud and long, but in the end he left the field and the game went on.

That was the beginning of a long round of trouble with the "Kid." He was a fighter on the field, and loved an argument; but off the diamond he was a great fellow and had a heart as big as a mountain. He helped a lot of people who were in trouble and said nothing about it. He was crazy about his family and they loved him devotedly.

* * *

I had a good deal of trouble in Little Rock that year due to the start I made by putting Elberfeld out of the park before the opening game had started.

One day I gave a close decision at home plate, and the bottles began to fly. I worked my way toward the dressing room, heads up to dodge the flying bottles. Several hit me, but none of them did any damage.

The chief of police and his wife were sitting in a car outside the gate waiting to take me to town. As I came out to get in, a crowd of several hundred were jammed around the car. The Chief's wife was frightened, but I assured her I had been in many a worse jam than this and that everything would be all right.

Later on the Chief and the "Kid" and I had a conference at the police station. I told the Chief I was going to run those ball games no matter how many times I got pop-bottled and that as long as Elberfeld gave me trouble I would keep putting him out of the park. The "Kid" was willing to listen to reason, and things quieted down considerably.

* * *

A thousand times I have been asked how I came to be called "Steamboat" Johnson. Up to the time I came into the Southern League, I was known as "Bulldog" Johnson.

On my first trip into Atlanta, Ga., in 1919, I was assigned to work behind the plate.

In those days before the loud speakers came into use, the umpire had to announce the batteries. After I had brushed off the plate, I called out the batteries in my usual voice, which I guess was pretty deep and loud.

Next day in the Atlanta *Georgian*, which is an

afternoon paper, Ed Danforth, the sporting editor, in writing up the game, said:

"None of us know where John D. Martin got this Umpire Johnson, but he has a voice like a Mississippi River steamboat. From now he is 'Steamboat' Johnson to Atlantans."

The name caught the ear of the public, and it has stuck to me ever since.

The Ty Cobb Incident

"Steamboat" Tells How He Forfeited Exhibition Game to Cardinals When Tiger Star Refused to Leave Game in Augusta, Ga., in 1923

I HANDLED all the exhibition games for Ty Cobb's Detroit Tigers in the spring of 1922. They were training in Augusta that year, and I got along fine.

The next spring I was engaged to handle the ten-game exhibition series between the Tigers and the St. Louis Cardinals that was to start in Augusta, April 7.

It was in that opening game in Augusta that I figured in an episode that created a lot of talk and still is mentioned in Augusta. It was then that I forfeited the first game of the exhibition series to St. Louis because Ty Cobb would not leave the game when ordered to do so by Cy Pfirman, my partner.

A big crowd had come in to see the game. Rogers Hornsby, champion batsman of the National League, and Cobb, the outstanding figure of the American League, were attractions that brought them in for miles around. The game was rocking along fine, and neither side had scored.

In the sixth inning with two out, Cobb singled and then tried to steal second. Umpire Pfirman, working the bases, called Cobb out.

Cobb leaped to his feet, scooped up a handful of dirt and threw it in Cy's face. Words were exchanged, and Pfirman ordered Cobb to leave the game.

Cobb refused and went out to his position in center field. Pfirman came over to me and said he had ordered Ty out. Then I walked out to center field and told Ty to leave, but he refused.

I told Cobb that I was in a terrible position because I knew that if I forfeited the game that he would fire me, and I would lose out on the exhibition series.

Cobb told me I was exactly right; that he would fire me if I forfeited the game.

I then told Cobb that if he had not left the game by the time I returned to home plate, I would forfeit the game to St. Louis. Ty warned me that if I forfeited the game the fans would mob me. I told him I would as soon be killed on a baseball field as anywhere else.

Some of the fans were yelling "Play ball." Others

were yelling at us umpires and some were yelling at Cobb to leave.

When I reached the plate, I looked around and Cobb was still there. So I took off my cap and announced to the stands that I forfeited the game to St. Louis because Manager Cobb had refused to leave the game when ordered to do so by Umpire Pfirman.

The fans came out on the field and crowded around us as we started away. They pushed and shoved us, and when we got to our dressing room, Pfirman found that all the buttons had been torn off his coat.

Pretty soon Manager Cobb came in and created a scene. He told me that I was fired and would not work the rest of the exhibition series. Then reporters came in and we told them that an exhibition game had to be run just like any other game, or else the public would lose interest. The promoters of the game called and asked if we could reverse the decision and start the game again, but we had to refuse.

Frank H. Barrett, owner of the Augusta club and of the ball park, then addressed the crowd and explained what had happened and ordered the admission money refunded.

The crowd stood outside and razzed us while we dressed. An old friend took us in his car to the Genesta Hotel, and we were not harmed physically at all.

Here is the box score of that forfeited game:

Detroit (A)	AB	H	O	A
Blue, 1b	3	0	8	0
Haney, 3b	3	0	1	1
Cobb, lf	3	1	1	0
Veach, rf	2	1	0	0
Heilman, cf	2	1	0	0
Pratt, 2b	2	0	0	2
Rigney, ss	2	0	1	3
Bassler, c	1	0	3	1
Collins, p	2	1	1	3
Totals	20	4	18	10

St. Louis (N)	AB	H	O	A
Blades, lf	3	0	2	0
Flack, rf	3	1	0	0
Hornsby, 2b	3	0	1	3
Bottomley, 1b	1	0	7	0
Stock, 3b	2	0	1	0
Meyers, cf	2	2	0	0
Freigau, ss	2	0	3	1
Clemens, c	2	0	4	1
Sherdel, p	2	0	0	2
Totals	20	3	18	7

St. Louis (N)	000 000—0
Detroit (A)	000 000—0

Stolen base—Heilman. Two-base hit—Heilman. Bases on balls—off Sherdel, 1; off Collins, 3. Struck out—by Sherdel, 2; by Collins, 3. Left on bases—St. Louis, 3; Detroit, 3. Passed balls—Bassler, Clemens. Double plays—Freigau to Hornsby; Bassler to Haney. Umpires—Johnson and Pfirman.

(Game forfeited to St. Louis 9 to 0 because of Cobb's refusal to leave the game after being ordered out by Umpire Pfirman at conclusion of sixth inning.)

The aftermath is the most interesting part of the story. I was down in the lobby paying my hotel bill and was going to catch a train for Memphis to attend a Southern League umpires' meeting. A telephone call came in for me. It was Cobb on the other end of the line. He said:

"I am sorry you made such a sad mistake out there this afternoon, but it all over now; so be at the station tonight when we leave. I want you to work the rest of the exhibition games for us."

I reminded Cobb that he had fired me a few hours before; but he told me to come along and finish out my contract, which I did.

We continued the trip, and when we reached Memphis, I sent word to Manager Cobb that I would like to drop off there, to which he agreed.

Wild Days in New Orleans

FIGHT WITH PITCHER CRAFT OVER LICORICE—PLAYERS RIOT IN 4-HOUR GAME—UMPIRES DEMAND RELEASE OF ARRESTED PLAYER—AND GET IT

NEW ORLEANS in the days of Jules Heinemann when baseball was at its height was a tough spot for umpires, and I have had my share of jams there.

One of the run-ins that I remember most clearly was when Bert Niehoff had the Mobile club going for a pennant.

Let me say right here that Niehoff is a smart capable manager, and as long as an umpire was hustling and keeping right on top of the play he would never give any trouble. Let an umpire give Bert the idea that he was asleep at the switch, or loafing on the job, and Bert could cause more trouble in five minutes than some of them could in a whole season.

Along in the middle of the game—it was a hot July afternoon—Bert came up to me and said—speaking of the New Orleans pitcher—"Steamboat, that fellow Craft is using something on the ball. Watch him.'

Next inning I saw Craft going back to his hip

pocket with his right hand, so I called time and ran out to the pitcher's box. Craft was standing there looking at me with his hands down at his side to see what I was going to do. I went behind him, reached into his pocket and brought out a long piece of licorice, such as small boys chew.

I said to Craft:

"You're out of the game," and turned and started for the plate. Just as I got to the plate, Craft had come up behind me. He grabbed me around the neck, and he was not trying to pet me, either. I was so surprised I could do nothing for a minute, but I finally managed to jerk loose.

I maneuvered until I was backed up against the backstop and was swinging my mask at his head, as he kept coming in and mixing it with me. By this time, four or five players crowded around and stopped the fight. Larry Gilbert put in another pitcher, and the game was finished.

A crowd milled around the dressing room after the game, but I was not harmed. They all thought Craft had tobacco in his pocket and was just reaching for a chew; but I knew better and, besides, had the licorice. I sent it in to President Martin with my report.

It was in Heinemann Park, August 27, 1927, that one of the longest nine inning games on record was played, and one of the worst fights occurred that I ever saw on any ball field. There were 15,411 people in the park. Some 2,000 broke down the gates after they had been closed by order of President Martin, who was there to see the game, and rushed in.

Along in the middle of the game Ray Gardner, New Orleans shortstop, was at bat. Hollis McLaughlin, the Birmingham pitcher, threw one so close to Gardner's head that Gardner took for a bean ball.

In a flash Gardner lost his temper and sailed out after McLaughlin.

Pel Ballenger, the Birmingham third baseman, rushed over to help Mac. They began to mix it up on the mound, and Joe Sonnenberg, a police captain who was at the game in civilian clothes, came out of the grandstand on the run to stop the fight. Max Rosenfeld, Birmingham second baseman, thought Sonneberg was a fan and met him with a solid lick to the jaw.

It was a fast, furious battle while it lasted, but the bluecoats stopped it and took Rosenfeld off to jail.

Umpires Brennan and Shannon and I, who were handling the game, told President Heinemann that we would not allow the game to be resumed until he got Rosenfeld out of jail, since the player had hit the police captain through a mistake. It took two hours to get Rosenfeld back from jail, and then we resumed play where we had left off.

The final score was 25 to 16 in favor of New Orleans. Fifteen two-base hits were made in all. The elapsed time from start to finish was 4 hours and 10 minutes.

Here is the official box score of that memorable game.

Birmingham	AB	R	H	PO	A	E
Ballenger, 3b	6	1	1	3	2	1
Gillis, ss	4	1	1	1	5	0
Ganzel, lf	6	3	3	1	0	0
Bigelow, rf	5	2	3	1	0	0
Yaryan, c	4	3	3	1	1	0
Hubert, c	1	0	0	0	0	0
Rosenfeld, 2b	4	0	2	1	3	1
Schepner, 2b	1	0	0	0	1	0
Barnes, cf	5	2	2	5	0	0
Jourdan, 1b	5	2	1	11	0	0
Brett, p	0	0	0	0	0	0
Newton, p	0	0	0	0	1	0
Coffman, p	3	1	2	0	0	0
McLaughlin, p	0	0	0	0	0	0
Kloza, p	2	1	1	0	0	0
Totals	46	16	19	24	13	2

New Orleans	AB	R	H	PO	A	E
Gardner, ss	5	3	2	2	4	1
Murray, ss	1	1	1	1	0	0
Blakesley, lf	5	4	4	2	0	0
Morgan, rf	5	4	4	1	0	1
Davis, 1b	3	5	2	14	0	0
Whitney, 3b	6	3	4	2	1	0
Vick, cf	6	1	5	2	0	0
Anderson, c	4	1	2	3	0	0
Ewoldt, 2b	6	1	1	0	6	1
Adkins, p	4	2	2	0	0	0
Martina, p	1	0	0	0	0	0
Totals	46	25	27	27	11	3

Score by innings:

Birmingham	010 022 533—16
New Orleans	310 404 130x—25

Summary: Two-base hits—Morgan, 2; Vick, 3; Adkins, Bigelow, 2; Yaryan, 3; Ganzel, 2; Whitney, Ballenger. Sacrifice hits—Anderson, Gillis, Martina. Left on bases—New Orleans, 8; Birmingham, 5. Base on balls—off Brett, 1; Martina, 1; Coffman, 5; Kloza, 1. Struck out—by Adkins, 1; Coffman, 1; Martina, 2. Hits—off Brett, 3 with 3 runs in 1-3 innings; Newton, 2 with 1 run in 3 innnings; Adkins, 12 with 10 runs in 6 2-3 innings; Coffman, 12 with 8 runs in 5 innings; McLaughline 6 with 9 runs in 1-3 inning. Wild pitches—McLaughlin, Kloza. Passed ball—Yaryan. Winning pitcher—Adkins. Losing pitcher—Brett. Umpires—Brennan, Shannon, Johnson. 4 hours and 10 minutes.

* * *

Late in the 1925 race Atlanta was playing in New Orleans. The game was close, and "Red" Torkelson, usually an easy-going sort of player, was at bat. A good strike came over and I called it.

Red turned around and said:

"Steamboat, that ball was not over the plate."

"It was," I said.

"Red" stepped out of the box and began calling me everything he could think of, and "Red" had an active mind.

"Out you go, Red," I said.

"You can't put me out," he said.

"But you already have been out a long time," I said, and so out he walked.

Then Buddy Rezza came to bat, and he took up where "Red" left off, looking back and talking to me.

I told him:

"It will cost you less to look at the pitcher than at me."

Well, Buddy stepped out of the box and talked himself out of the game. That made two in all, and I knew I was in for it.

On my way to the dressing room I got a pop-bottle shower. The police rallied around and took the bottle shower, too, just to see that I got safely off the field. The crowd waited for me outside the park, so Superintendent of Police Mooney, since deceased, took me down to the police station in his car and several hours later took me to the Hotel Monteleon where the umpires were stopping.

* * *

Another time when Buck Campbell and I were working in New Orleans, Taylor, the Birmingham catcher, spiked the New Orleans second baseman when he slid into the base. The New Orleans players rushed up and claimed Taylor interfered with the play, but I could not see anything wrong and refused to call him out.

After that game was over we were not so lucky at dodging bottles. I stopped one with my jaw, and I was lucky the bottle did not break. Campbell was hit twice on the ankle. The Birmingham club had to stay on their bench a long time until the excitement had died down before they could take the chance of walking past the end of the grandstand.

It was that experience that led the New Orleans management to build a concrete tunnel under the grandstand, so players would not have to come in contact with fans after the game.

* * *

The New Orleans police force always has been active in trying to catch bottle throwers and always have been ready to give umpires or players protection. Conditions have improved now, due to the sportsmanship of Larry Gilbert, president and manager of the club. Manager Gilbert is one of the finest men in baseball and a credit to the profession. He practices the Golden Rule in giving visiting teams and the umpires every assistance and protection.

* * *

The Southern League has had a number of the grandest men in baseball come and go during the time I have been umpiring. I was fortunate to have come in contact with them and always will remember them for the many courtesies they have shown.

No league ever lost finer men than Jules Heinemann, of New Orleans; Charlie Frank, of Atlanta; Sammy (Strang) Nicklin, of Chattanooga; Wilbert

Robinson, of Atlanta; and W. D. Smith, of Birmingham. They were club presidents of the highest caliber. Their successors are following in their footsteps which goes to make the Southern League the best minor league in America.

HOW TO WATCH THE PLATE

"The Steamer" shows the correct form here for working behind the plate. Gerard Lipscomb is leading off for the Crackers, Lee Head catching for Knoxville in the opener (1935) in Atlanta before the record crowd of 18,671.

PARTNERS FOR FIVE YEARS

"'Andsome 'Arry" Campbell (left) and "Steamboat" Johnson worked Southern League ball games together for five years, said to be a record for two umpires in any minor league.

'Way Down South

CIVIL VS. BASEBALL LAW—CHARLIE FRANK TAKES OUT INJUNCTION AGAINST MOBILE PITCHER—ATLANTA STAGED BIGGEST BOTTLE SHOWER

SOMETIMES constables and other officers of the law come into the baseball field to discharge their duties, and that is where an umpire is really up against it. I am not sure what a court would say about which one had more authority, but I guess it goes with the side that can talk faster.

Mobile was playing in Atlanta one day during the time Charlie Frank was manager of the Crackers. It was the last game of the series, and both teams were catching a train right after the game.

Bob Hasty was pitching for Mobile, and the game was going along fine, when a man in plain clothes came walking out toward the pitcher's mound.

I immediately called time and rushed out to see what the man wanted. He stated that he was the law, showed me his badge and a warrant for Hasty.

Charlie Frank had taken out an injunction in court to keep Hasty from pitching! It was just another trick of the foxy Frank.

"You have no right on this field," I said. "I am running this game and will stand for no interference from the law or anything else."

The officer told me I could not put him out of the park.

"But I can forfeit the game to the visiting club," I replied. "And I will do that thing right now, if you do not go back in the grandstand."

The officer then said he would wait outside and get Hasty when the game was over.

In some way, exact details of which I never learned, Hasty slipped out of the park by a side gate, into a taxicab and rushed down to the station where he was locked in a drawing room on the Mobile pullman car. None of us ever heard of that warrant again.

Another time, Mobile was playing Chattanooga when First Baseman Knode got into an argument with a fan in the stand. A policeman came out and put the sleeve on Knode and was about to take him off the field.

I rushed over and interfered, using the same argument I had used in Atlanta about forfeiting the game to the visiting club if spectators interfered with the play. The policeman went back in the stand, promising to arrest Knode immediately after the game.

I was in the dressing room just getting into my street clothes when the officer appeared at the door.

"I have a warrant for you for interfering with an officer in the discharge of his duty," he said.

"You can't do that," I said. "I was running that ball game."

"Well, read this warrant and see whether you think I can or not," he replied.

I read the warrant, and that is exactly what it said.

The officer told me he would trust me to report at nine o'clock and see the Judge about it. I was there on time next morning, and the Judge told me to make the players keep quiet and not jaw with fans in the stands. I told him it was hard to do, but I would try. So both Knode and I were dismissed with a warning.

* * *

It was in Little Rock in 1920 that I got into a complicated mix-up with a fan in the grandstand.

Carleton Molesworth had his Birmingham club in there that day, and along in the latter part of the game I called a Birmingham player safe on a close play at the plate. A fan in the stand right back of the plate began calling me all the names in the book. I paid no attention, but went on with the game. Then the fan turned on Manager Molesworth, and began to abuse him in a highly personal way.

"Moley" came up to me and said:

"Steamboat, this can't go on. Have that fan put out of the park."

I promised I would if I heard any more from him. In the ninth inning the man started up again on Molesworth; so I went over to the Little Rock bench and told the "Kid" to have a policeman take the man out of the park.

"Put him out yourself if he is worrying you and Moley," the "Kid" said.

Molesworth insisted I put him out.

"Let me see how much nerve you have got, Steamboat," he argued.

So I went up to where the fan was sitting and said:

"If you do not leave the park, I will forfeit the game to Birmingham."

By that time the "Kid" came over and said he would have the man put out. He gave a sign to a plain clothes man, and soon the fan was on his way and the game was finished in peace.

As often as not managers and players came to our assistance when the bottles began to fly, especially home town managers, because they knew we could forfeit the game if it became impossible to continue play in safety.

One afternoon in Memphis on my second trip around the circuit Birmingham was the opposition, and a great crowd was on hand.

Early in the game I had to chase Catcher Meyers, of the Memphis club, for abusing me. No sooner did Meyers start for the showers than the bottles began to fly. They came thick and fast and collided in mid-air and broke in pieces around the plate. One or two hit me on the shoulder and several hit my legs.

Manager John McCloskey, of Memphis, rushed out and faced the crowd. He raised his arms and yelled at them to quit throwing bottles, or the game would be forfeited to Birmingham. The crowd quieted down. Players and groundkeepers began picking up bottles from the infield, and after fifteen minutes play was resumed. Bill Brennan and Cy Pfirman were working with me that day, and President Martin was a spectator.

* * *

But of all the bottle showers I ever ran into the biggest was in Atlanta, a city in which fans are usually very orderly and treat umpires and players fairly.

It was on a holiday and Mobile was playing. In the eleventh inning of the game, I had to put Bob Higgins, catcher, and Ray Roberts, pitcher, both out of the game at once. The sight of an umpire firing their battery all at once infuriated the fans. There were around 15,000 present, and it looked as if every one must have had a bottle in his hand. For here came a shower of bottles that beat anything I ever experienced.

The Atlanta fans were good throwers too. I was hit several times in the head and in the back, but fortunately I was not knocked out. The police took me to the dressing room under the grandstand.

There was a window right above the shower bath, and as I stepped in and turned on the water somebody fired a pistol outside. The bullet broke the glass and flattened against the wall.

It happened that when the shot was fired I was bending down washing my feet, so it missed my head. Otherwise I might not be writing these lines now.

The police, who were standing-by inside the room, ran outside, but in the crowd of several hundred they could not locate who had fired the shot. Neither were the officers able to break up the crowd, so they took me out the back gate, and I arrived at the Oliver Hotel with no more adventures.

The first man to talk to me after I arrived at the hotel was Bill Cody, the chief of the fire department, now departed. Chief Cody was a fine sportsman, and he came in to apologize for the way Atlanta fans had treated me, but I told him I held no resentment toward them at all.

The Umpire—A Lonely Chap

Day's Routine and Custom Bars Friendly Contacts—What He Does Each Hour—"Steamboat" Tells Just What He Says in a Game

FEW fans have any idea of the life an umpire leads during the season. Let me give you the routine of a typical day. Then maybe you will be satisfied to work in an office or a store and not envy us our hours—3 to 5—which are supposed to be good ones.

In most leagues, as in the Southern League, two umpires travel together. We arrive in town on an early train. On leaving the train we look closely after our bags. They contain our tools, as we call our equipment, such as mask, protectors and so on. Without our tools we could not work.

Then we take a cab to our hotel. It is always a different hotel from the one at which the ball players stop. There is no rule about this, but the unwritten law of the profession. Anyone can see that it never would do for umpires to be seen fraternizing with ball players.

On assignment to our room, the first thing is to unpack the damp, sweaty clothes in which we worked the day before, and dry them. We also send our suits out to be pressed, since an umpire always must look neat.

We have breakfast at about 9:30 o'clock. We return immediately to our room and relax. We lie down and sleep or read until an hour or so before the game.

Few umpires ever eat lunch. That helps keep their heads clear on the field. This also is done to avoid contacts with friends. It is better that we do so, especially in towns where we know a great many people.

An hour before game time, we pack up our tools and go to the park. We proceed at once to the dressing room and get ready for the day's work.

Just what an umpire wears may surprise many fans. Most of us prepare for a game in about the same way with only slight variations, and I will give you my method of dressing.

First I put on three-quarter length heavy woolen socks. They are easier on the feet and absorb perspiration. Then I put on my shoes and tie the laces carefully. An umpire's shoes should never come unfastened.

Next come the shin protectors. These are narrow and much lighter than those worn by the catcher and have extensions that protect the ankles.

Next is a heavy sweat shirt—some umpires use a

light cotton shirt—and then the chest protector. The new style of protector is made of fiber and is light. It is designed to wear under the coat and is very compact with sponge rubber pads next to the ribs and over the shoulder blades.

The pants are put on next. I wear suspenders when working behind the plate because in stooping down so often to see balls and strikes, the pants are likely to slip out of place and destroy a neat appearance. Then I put on my coat and cap, and sit down to relax.

About this time the home club sends in eighteen balls for us to take charge of and inspect. Four of them are new balls and fourteen almost new ones, or alternate balls. We look at these carefully to see that they have not been tampered with. Defective balls are thrown out and others called for.

In three to five minutes before game time, I pick up my mask, which is made of heavy wire or steel of the open vision type, and take up the small grip in which the balls are carried. I make sure that my whiskbroom is in one hip pocket—an umpire would be lost without a whiskbroom to brush off the plate—and likewise to see that the indicator is in another pocket. In company with my partner, I go at once to the field.

The above details of dressing and preparation are given in case I am working behind the plate. A base umpire wears no protectors of any sort and has no use for a whiskbroom or indicator. In summer, he may go without his coat in the Southern League at his discretion.

Arriving in the neighborhood of the plate, I open the grip of balls and take out six or eight. These I put into the pockets of my coat and put the grip out of the way against the backstop.

Umpires working behind the plate now wear coats in all seasons because of convenience in carrying balls. The old custom of carrying the balls in a blouse has about disappeared.

Then I call the managers of the two teams to the plate. Both umpires participate in the conference over ground rules. After these details are fixed, the base umpire takes his place. I brush off the plate, hand a new ball to the catcher, and put on my mask. I may say here that most umpires nowadays wear the cap with visor forward and do not turn it backward as was formerly the custom, and still is with catchers.

Then I take the indicator in my hand (usually the left) see that it is set at zero for balls and strikes and call "Play."

When the game is over, we umpires leave the field as rapidly as possible. We do not stop to talk to friends. Even when an old acquaintance speaks, we return his greeting, but keep right on walking.

It is considered bad business to stop and shake hands with a friend. It might cause fans to wonder whether that man had placed a bet on the game and was thanking us for helping him win. It sounds far-fetched, but it is very important. I have hurt the feelings of some of my best friends by not shaking hands or stopping to talk when leaving the field, and have had to explain it to them afterward.

We undress and take a shower, then dress and go at once to our hotel. There we fill out a report card for that game. The card has blanks for the date, home team, visiting team, weather conditions, ground conditions, time game started, time it finished, and remarks on conduct of players, fines imposed, players sent out of the game and anything else of an unusual nature. Included also are spaces for the name of our hotel, our next assignment and finally the names of the umpires. This card is mailed to headquarters, where it becomes a part of the records of the league.

After making our report we have dinner, our second and last meal of the day. We usually dine in a quiet restaurant and try to dine alone. Occasionally friends invite us out to their homes for dinner and that is a real treat.

After dinner we usually go back to our hotel. Attending the movies sometimes hurts our eyes because squinting into the glare of the sun all day often makes our eyes very tired. At the hotel, we read and go to bed early. When our assignment ends in that town, we go on to the next and repeat the process from April until October.

An umpire leads a lonely life. He has few human contacts save with his partner. He is as isolated as a monk in a monastery. At the end of the season, he is glad to get into some business like operating a restaurant or working in a department store or a filling station where he can have human contacts and talk to as many people as possible.

In these days of big ball parks not all the fans can hear what the umpire says to indicate his decisions to the players. Every umpire has his code, so I will give you mine.

To start the game I cry "Play," not "Play Ball," and I raise my arm above my head with fists closed. To halt the game I call "Time," and raise one hand.

On strikes I call "Strike—ah—one" and put the right arm outward with one finger extended; "Strike—ah—two" and put the right arm out with two fingers extended; "Strike—ah—three, you're out."

On balls I call "Ball one," but do not give a hand signal. Then I say "That's two" on the second ball; "That's three" on the third ball; "That's four," on the fourth.

I never say "Take your base." I let him figure that out for himself.

If the pitcher calls for the count, I put out both arms indicating the number of strikes with the right fingers and the number of balls with the left fingers. I always watch the scoreboard so I can correct errors there with hand signals.

A base umpire says nothing to start the game. He cannot call time, but signals to the umpire behind the plate if he wants it called.

The uniform signal for calling a runner "safe" on the bases is both hands extended palms down. The signal for "out" is the right arm jerked up and back thumb extended.

My own addition to the hand signal for "out" is to cry "No! No!"

What the players say to us and what we say in return cannot be set down in this book.

Brothers in Blue

SCOTTY CHESTNUT, A COLORFUL UMPIRE—LETS BATTER CALL A BALL—DAN PFENNINGER'S WIT —BILL BRENNAN ALWAYS HAD AN ANSWER READY

NO more colorful umpire ever worked in the Southern League than Scott Chestnut, now connected with the Paramount Pictures Corporation in the Southern territory.

Scotty ran the game from beginning to end and always had an answer ready for any ball player who felt talkative. He backed it up with the best pair of eyes in the business and could see a base play as good as any man I ever saw.

Once upon a time the umpires were stopping at the old Kimball House in Atlanta, which also was a sort of headquarters for members of the legislature, then in session. Scotty was sitting in the lobby watching the legislators moving around. I came up for a chat, and he said:

"Steamboat, let's talk fake foreign lingo out loud and see what these boys from down in the country think about it.'

So I sat down by him, and we began jabbering at each other in no language at all. Pretty soon the legislators crowded around listening to us carry on that phony conversation, and finally one of them said to Scotty:

"Mister, you sure can talk Chinese. Would you mind telling me what you are saying?"

Scotty had the nerve to get away with things the average umpire never would think of trying. He was working behind the plate one day when Chattanooga was playing in New Orleans. "Red" Blume, a great fellow, was the New Orleans first baseman then, and "Red" was at bat. The count was two and two.

As the next pitch came down the alley, a gust of wind blew dust into Scotty's eyes.

"How did the ball look to you, Red?" Scotty asked.

"It looked like a ball," Red replied.

"Ball three," Scotty called.

The Chattanooga catcher turned around and yelled:

"For Pete's sake, who ever heard of an umpire letting a ball player call 'em. How do you get that way?"

Scotty replied:

"Because I have always found Mr. Blume to be a man of high integrity."

The Chattanooga catcher was not sure what Scotty meant, and went on with his beefing:

"Well, all I ask is that when I am up there hitting and the bases are full and we need one run to win and the count is three and two, you let me call the next one."

"I will," said Scotty, "as soon as you prove to me you are half the man Mr. Blume is."

Up came the next pitch and Scotty called the batter out.

Manager Johnny Dobbs came rushing up to the plate and told Scotty the ball was a foot outside and said to Blume:

"Wasn't it outside, Red?"

Red came right back with:

"No, Johnny, it was right down the middle."

For some reason or other, Munce Pigue had a tough time through his short career as a Southern League umpire. Why? I cannot understand it as he was a fine, sincere man who knew baseball and called 'em as he saw 'em.

One day in Memphis in 1924, Munce was working behind the plate with Bill Brennan and Dan Pfenninger on the bases. Atlanta was the visiting club. Guy Morton was pitching for Memphis and did not like the way Munce was calling balls and strikes. Morton began arguing and words came thick and fast. Finally Pigue ordered Morton out of the game. Morton refused to go, so Munce courageously forfeited the game to Atlanta 9 to 0.

That was the signal for a bottle shower and the umpires had a time getting to their dressing rooms.

It so happened that a friend of mine knew I was passing through town on my way to Little Rock, so he called me at home where Lou Jorda and I were just eating supper and told me that we had better hurry to the park as the crowd was after the umpires and was going to lynch them.

So Lou and I hurried to the park and the crowd warned us not to go inside or we would get the same medicine they were planning to dish out to the three who had worked the game. We got inside and found that none of the three was hurt. The police took us out the back gate and all of us escaped.

Munce Pigue would have made a good umpire, but he decided to go back to the newspaper business in which he had been successful before and in which he is successful now.

Dan Pfenninger was a grand old man, who served the Southern League well as an umpire and stood the gaff like a man from beginning to end. His retirement took a fine character away from the ball field.

Old Dan had a ready wit that pulled him out of many a jam with the players.

One day a heavy-hitting batsman, after missing two healthy swings a mile, stood there and let a fast ball slip right down the middle without offering to hit it.

"Strike three," Dan called.

"You missed one that time, Dan," the player protested.

"But you just missed two," Dan came back. "So I'm better than you are."

When the player reached the bench, he repeated the wisecrack and said: "How could you get mad at a man like that?"

* * *

The late Bill Brennan was a man who upheld the dignity of the profession at all times and was well-nigh perfect in calling them. Bill could handle players better than almost any man I ever worked with. I was with him in many important games when pennant races were close and in several Dixie series play-offs and always found him master of the situation.

Bill stopped a ball player in Birmingham when working the bases. He called the player out on a close one at second.

After the player had dusted himself off, he continued to rave. Bill called "play" and the player shouted:

"Bill, I demand my rights."

Brennan came back with:

"Trot to your position before I hand you a couple of lefts."

* * *

Polly McLarry, now a Southern League umpire, tells this one that was pulled on him in Des Moines on the occasion of the first night game in that city. Jimmy Payton, then managing the Pueblo Club, handed him the batting order. It read:

Paul Revere, centerfield; Al Capone, leftfield; Jack Fleagle, second base; Earl Carroll, shortstop; Charles Lindbergh, rightfield; Harry K. Thaw, third base; Jesse James, first base; Paul Whiteman, catcher; Cole Younger, pitcher; Daniel Boone scout; Texas Guinan, hostess.

* * *

Umpire Jack Gifford, after finishing his talk with the managers about ground rules in Nashville, took out his whiskbroom and began brushing the dirt off home plate.

Jack brushed and brushed, but no plate appeared. A ball player, the first hitter, watched him a minute, then pointed with his bat and said:

"Here is the plate over here."

Gifford then saw he was several feet away from where the plate really was. Ever after that the players who were in that game always razzed him by calling him "Home Plate" Gifford.

* * *

One of the finest young umpires who ever broke into the Southern League is Claude Bond, an Atlanta boy, who was assigned to me in 1935 as a partner. Claude made good from the jump. He is a fast worker, has good judgment, a fine disposition, is big and strong and can stand the gaff. Bond is sure to go higher in his chosen profession. Good young umpires are hard to find, but he is one of the best.

* * *

I think the Southern League has had the best umpires of any minor league in the country, especially since John D. Martin became president. Good umpires are hard to find. There is a saying that there are a thousand good umpires in the winter, but only a few in the summer. That means that many call themselves umpires, but few of them are chosen.

It has been said that all the good umpires have jobs. That comes about because every league wants to keep its own umpires, especially if they are experienced men, and hesitate to change from year to year. A league president hesitates to try out an umpire unless the applicant has had years of experience and good recommendations.

I say that the Southern League has good umpires

for every one of them who went to the majors has made good. Cy Pfirman, Bill McGowan, Lou Jorda, Bill Brennan, Bick Campbell and John Quinn are a few of them who went to the majors by way of the Southern.

The umpires in the Texas League are all tiptop men too, due to the careful selections made by Alvin Gardner, one of the finest characters and one of the best presidents in minor league baseball.

All Purely Personal

UMBRELLA WOMAN ATTACKS—A DOCTOR "GETS TOLD"—GOOD EYESIGHT DEMONSTRATED—FASTEST GAME—THE EARTHQUAKE IN LOS ANGELES

ONE day in New Orleans, I had just finished a game that had given me a lot of close decisions to call against the home club and they had lost. The fans were booing us as we left the field. Under the grandstand where we had to pass on our way to the dressing room, a crowd gathered and, as we walked through, a lady came up behind me.

Before I realized what was happening, she had begun to hit me over the head with her umbrella, one lick after another. I defended myself as best I could and said:

"Lady, I don't know who you are, but if you get someone to introduce us, you can go on hitting me."

She was surprised, put her umbrella down and laughed.

* * *

A doctor, sitting in a box close to the playing field in Nashville was razzing me every time he thought I missed one. Finally I turned around and yelled:

"Doctor, they bury all your mistakes."

And all the fans who heard it just roared and the doctor laid off of me from then on.

* * *

Nashville fans got on us hot and heavy one afternoon and after the game a crowd of them came around to our dressing room and challenged us to come outside. I went to the door, in my street clothes, and made a bluff at my hip pocket and yelled:

"Just wait until I get this gun out and you'll leave us alone."

The fans scattered in every direction, not knowing that I have never carried a gun, only that long snap blade knife.

* * *

During the summer of 1935, when New Orleans was playing in Atlanta, I called the third strike on Eddie Rose, of New Orleans. He turned to me, leaned the bat up against my leg and said:

"Steamboat, you take the bat and see if you can reach a ball that was as far outside as that one."

So I replied:

"Take your bat, Eddie, and go on into the club house and see if you can take a good shower."

Well, Eddie went on and I suppose he took the shower.

One day a few years ago I was working in New Orleans and stopping at the Hotel Monteleon. I came into the lobby and noticed several ball players looking on the floor for something. I went over and said:

"Boys, have you lost something?"

They said:

"Yes, Steamboat, we are looking for a diamond pin, but you are blind and can't help us."

"Stand back," I said, "and I'll find it."

I looked around and saw it in the crack between two of the granite blocks of the lobby floor.

"Now don't any of you call me blind this afternoon in the game, or it will cost you the price of that pin."

* * *

Five years ago, President John D. Martin was in Chattanooga attending a game that I was working. On returning to my hotel, the Read House, I met him coming out. He said he was on his way to catch a train and I went along with him to see him off.

The station is right across the street from the Read House and when less than five minutes were left before the train was scheduled to leave he discovered he had forgotten his Gladstone bag. I offered to run back and get it, and lit out.

I ran into the lobby of the hotel and looked over the long line of grips and picked his out by the initials

"J. D. M." stamped in small gold letters on it. I hurried back and handed the bag to Mr. Martin as he was standing on the steps of the moving train. He asked me how I knew which was his bag and I told him by the initials.

"Harry," he said, "I'll never have to get a certificate from an eye doctor for you. Your eyes are good to have picked that one out."

* * *

Just in case fans argue with me about my eyesight I carry a certificate made out by a recognized oculist and frequently renewed, which says that my left eye is 20-20, right eye 20-20, according to army tests.

* * *

Fans have asked me to pick an all-star Southern League team for 1935. Here is one that is a matter of personal opinion from the umpire's position:

Taitt, Nashville, left field.
Weatherly, New Orleans, center field.
Gleason, New Orleans, right field.
Lewis, Chattanooga, third base.
Rodda, Nashville, shortstop.
Mihalic, Chattanooga, second base.
Hooks, Atlanta, first base.
Gooch, Nashville, catcher.
Autry, New Orleans, catcher.
Kelley, Atlanta, pitcher.
Chaplin, Nashville, pitcher.
Milnar, New Orleans, pitcher.
Eiland, Nashville, pitcher.

Out in the Western League—"old 101 Ranch"—I was working one Fourth of July when a lot of cowboys were in from the range and sitting in the bleachers.

The score was tied in the ninth and bases were loaded. The batter lifted a high fly to left field and the cowboys playfully drew their pistols and shot the ball to pieces before it came down. They frightened the outfielders to death and all three runs scored. I may say that I did not call that one against the home team.

* * *

The fastest game of baseball I have ever worked was in Binghampton, N. Y., in the New York State League in 1917, which was run off in only 57 minutes. The shortest one in that league was handled by Connie Lewis, a great fellow and a good umpire.

The story of Umpire Lewis and his fast game can be told in two notes we wrote. After my 57-minute game was done, I dropped Connie a line telling him how I had gotten the Wilkesbarre and Binghampton players to hustle one off for me and give me the league record.

"That's how fast I am in my old age," I said.

After the season was over I received this letter from Connie:

"Friend Harry: I realized all along that you were fast, so I waited until the last game of the season to beat you. Syracuse and Scranton played one for me yesterday in 46 minutes. I waited until the last because I knew if I gave you a chance you would have run one off in three-quarters of an hour."

The box score of that Syracuse-Scranton game Connie worked follows:

Scranton	AB	R	H	PO	A	E
Murphy, lf	4	1	0	0	0	0
McCabe, p, cf	3	0	0	2	0	1
Brannan, c	3	0	1	3	2	0
Gazella, 2b	3	0	0	5	2	1
Walsh, ss	3	0	0	4	2	0
Gilpin, cf, rf	3	0	1	1	0	1
Higgins, 1b	3	0	1	9	2	0
Meyers, rf, p	3	0	0	0	2	0
Delaney, 3b	3	0	0	0	4	0
Totals	28	1	3	24	14	3

Syracuse	AB	R	H	PO	A	E
Madden, 1b	4	2	2	12	0	0
Keating, 2b	3	2	2	2	7	0
Riley, cf	2	2	1	1	0	0
O'Neill, lf	4	1	2	0	0	0
Konnick, ss	3	1	1	4	5	0
Burke, 3b	3	0	0	1	2	2
Williams, c	4	0	1	2	2	0
Friel, rf	4	0	0	4	0	0
Karpp, p	3	0	0	1	2	0
Totals	30	8	9	27	18	2

Score by innings:

Scranton	100 000 000—1
Syracuse	310 010 30x—8

Summary: Two-base hits—Madden, O'Neil, Keating, Higgins. Stolen bases—Madden, 3; Keating, 2. Earned runs—Syracuse, 4. Sacrifice hit—McCabe. Double plays—Burke to Keating to Madden; Meyers to Higgins to Brannan. Left on bases—Scranton, 2; Syracuse, 3. First base on errors—Scranton, 2; Syracuse, 1. Bases on balls—Off McCabe, 3; off Meyers, 1. Hits—Off McCabe, 1 in 1 inning; off Karpp, 3 in 9 innings; off Meyers, 8 in 7 innings. Hit by pitched ball—By McCabe (Burke). Struck out—By Karpp, 1. Time of game—46 minutes.

* * *

You can throw out all the jams I have encountered on the ball field as just so much fun compared to my experience in the earthquate in Los Angeles in March, 1933.

I was with the Giants at their spring training camp in Los Angeles and we had just returned to the Biltmore Hotel after playing an exhibition game with the Cubs at Wrigley Field.

I had just arrived in my room when I felt the building begin to rock. The floor swayed under my feet like a boat does and the pictures on the walls swayed.

People began screaming all over the place and I heard them rushing out into the halls.

I looked out of the window and could not believe my eyes when I saw the Commonwealth-Edison Building and the City Hall rocking from side to side. I could neither move nor talk and heretofore I had never had any trouble doing either, rapidly.

After the hotel stopped shaking for a minute, I

realized what had been happening, and I ran into the halls and started down the stairs. The halls and stairs were crowded with frightened people. Downstairs in the lobby some of the Cubs and Giants were gathered looking at the chandeliers sway.

Most of them, however, were across the street in the middle of the park which after all looked like the only safe place. That was one time I did not hesitate to join up with the players out in public, although I did not have much to say.

A Year in the Sally

ONCE A SAILOR, ALWAYS A SAILOR—BALL PLAYERS WERE A WILD LOT—SEES GOOSE GOSLIN GO UP —CITES TWO GOOD BASEBALL SCOUTS

SOUTHERN League fans often ask where I was in 1921. I went over to the South Atlantic League that year, and what a time I had! The players that year had the idea they could frighten any umpire they wanted to, but they found me an umpire who had worked in the "101 Ranch" and did not frighten easily.

W. W. Walsh was president of the league, and he always backed up his umpires. However, umpires were coming and going that year in the Sally, for not all of them could take it.

The toughest town in the league, I believe, was Charleston, S. C. They gave you plenty to think about over there.

I remember one day I was working with Jack Hoey, a fine partner and as game as they come. Jack had been a sailor during the war and had been discharged with the rating of Chief Boatswain's Mate. He knew all the seagoing language, which I can assure you gives a man a lot of words to say when he is in a corner.

That day the bleachers were full of sailors who were on shore leave from the fleet that was in the harbor. Jack had passed a few remarks to them in seagoing language, and they knew he was one of them.

Jack was working behind the plate, and late in the game he called a close one against the home team. The home fans started to come out of the stands after Jack, but Jack yelled something to the sailors. They came pouring out of the bleachers and drove the fans back into the grandstand. The game went on, and at the finish not a soul bothered us.

I asked Jack what he had said to the sailors that made them stand by him; and he answered, "All hands on deck."

* * *

It was in Columbia, S. C., one day that Manager Zinn Beck threw his bat at the pitcher who had just dusted him off, as we say when a pitcher throws at a batter's head. Zinn not only threw his bat at the pitcher, but went out after him. I got to the mound almost as soon as Beck did and put him out of the game for throwing his bat. I learned later on that after the game the ball players had a big fight, but

"YOU'RE OUT"

"Steamboat" Johnson demonstrates correct form in calling Krehmyer, of Atlanta, out at first while First Baseman Knode, of Mobile, looks around for the answer.

A CLOSE ONE AT NIGHT

"Steamboat" Johnson is right on top of this one at third base as Johnny Hill, of Atlanta, slides into the bag, while Manager Eddie Moore (No. 1) looks on.

that did not concern me, as an umpire's responsibility ends when the game is over.

Clark Griffith, of the Washington club, was in the stands that day looking at a player called "Goose" Goslin, and a few days later Goslin was signed by Washington.

Eddie Herr also was there scouting for Detroit and looking at a young shortstop named Tavener whom he later bought.

Herr is one of the best scouts I have ever seen. He was not the type to grab off a ball player in a hurry after seeing him go good in one or two games. He would follow a good prospect around for weeks and weeks and check him carefully in every respect. Pat Flaherty was another scout of the Eddie Herr type who knows a ball player and never takes snap judgment.

My contract with the Sally League had a clause making me a free agent when the season was over. I really enjoyed working for President Walsh and liked most of the towns in the league, but I was anxious to get back in the Southern. At the winter meeting that year in Buffalo, I had a long talk with President Martin and then and there signed a contract to return to the Southern. I have been there ever since, and intend to stay on as long as President Martin wants me and my health holds out. He is an ideal league president and the factor that has made the Southern League pre-eminent among the minors.

* * *

Four times I have been on exhibition tours with the Detroit Tigers, twice with the Giants and once with the Cleveland Indians.

* * *

I have umpired in the Dixie series seven times.

* * *

Each year I have received hundreds of letters from managers, ball players and fans from all parts of the country asking for rulings on freak plays.

* * *

I have never used tobacco nor liquor in my life.

* * *

There were 2,675 ball players under contract in organized baseball in 1935.

* * *

No umpire in the entire history of baseball has ever been charged with or found guilty of any serious act of dishonesty or corruption.

* * *

An umpire must render about 275 decisions in every ball game.

* * *

There are only 150 umpires in the United States under contract in organized baseball. Few will believe that there are so few.

Every town in the Southern League at one time or another has treated me to a pop bottle shower.

* * *

My count shows I have umpired over 4,000 games in 25 years.

* * *

I have rendered about 1,000,000 decisions since I began umpiring in 1909.

* * *

Something like 4,000 bottles have been thrown at me in my day, but only about 20 ever hit me. That does not speak very well for the accuracy of fans' throwing.

* * *

My umpiring assignments have taken me 40,000 miles.

* * *

One of my most prized assignments was umpiring a game between an all-star team of old-timers and the Los Angeles club for the benefit of the Association of Ball Players and Umpires of America in Los Angeles.

In One Easy Lesson

"Steamboat" Tells Young Umpires How to Start Right—Instructions Constitute Textbook on Umpiring—Maintain Dignity off the Field

YOUNG umpires just starting out or men who have been working only a short time may derive some benefit from a few hints that I will give here. Unless he is determined to make good in the profession, unless he is firm by nature, unless he is a student of human nature and can size up men quickly, unless he is willing to bear no malice but make his decisions impersonally at all times—and above all —unless he resolves not to have "rabbit ears" and not to listen to what is said in the grandstand, a man had better try some other profession than that of umpiring.

I always tell young umpires to provide themselves with good equipment and see that it is in good working order. Careful selection of your tools is necessary before you can do good work.

The protector that is worn under the coat is the best style to use. It does not interfere with your movements and is light and therefore does not tire you out. The shin guards and protectors for the instep should be the best make and light as possible so you can get about fast to keep up with the play.

The first thing you do when you come into the playing field is to go to the plate and call the managers of each club. Never go to their dugouts, as that lowers the dignity of the profession and looks too intimate to the fans who are sure to be watching.

Ask each manager for his batting order.

Then take up the ground rules. You want to be dead sure that everybody has a clear understanding of ground rules, for a misunderstanding of what is not in the book can cause more trouble than all the book rules put together. Do all you can to have as few ground rules as possible.

Look carefully to see that the foul lines are clearly visible out to the fences.

See that first and third bags are in line and keep watching them as the game goes along. These two spots will get you in trouble when you least expect it, as so many hits are driven down the foul lines. The bases, if in place, are a great help in determining whether the ball is fair or foul.

Keep hustling at all times and make the players hustle. Always have your next hitter ready, as that will speed up the game. Inspire the players with confidence in your decisions.

When working behind the plate be careful of your position. When a left-handed batter is up, stand over to the right a little bit so you can see the inside pitch. When a right-hand batter is up, stand a little to the left. Bend down to follow low pitches, as you cannot judge them when standing erect.

Never try to guess what the next pitch will be.

Keep your eye on the ball from the moment it leaves the pitcher's hand until it hits the catcher's glove or is struck by the batter. Never take your eye off for a moment.

Never call your decisions on balls and strikes too quickly. That goes also for decisions on the bases. Be sure you are right, then don't hesitate.

When umpiring the bases, be sure to follow up all tag plays, for the fielder may drop the ball after he has touched the runner. If you turn away too soon, it may get you into a shower of bottles.

Watch both the ball and the runner in a chase between the bases. The runner will try to fool you by ducking out of line. You are the sole judge of whether he went three feet out of line or not.

Run as close to a trapped ball play as you can. It is an easy one for you to miss. Many balls hit on a line to the outfield are caught close to the ground;

and unless you are close on it, it is hard to tell whether it was a shoestring catch or a trapped ball.

One good way to judge this sort of play is like this: If the fielder comes up quickly with the ball, it is a sure shot he made a clean catch of it; but when he hesitates, as a man will do to be sure he has trapped the ball, you are safe in ruling it no catch.

No matter how you rule on a play of this sort, you are sure to hear a lot of squawking.

The best position to stand for umpiring the bases is to the left of the pitcher's mound. That is the best angle from which to see a play from the pitcher to catch a man off first.

When a double play is on, you can run quickly to second base and have a good angle for the play at first as well. Getting into position for a double play requires quick starting and heads up all the way.

When a man is on third, none or one out, and the double system of umpiring is in use, move over behind third base to be ready for the runner to try to score after an outfield fly is caught. Unless you are right on the spot, you cannot judge whether the runner left before the catch was made or not.

The toughest spot for a base umpire is when men are on first and second and none out. Get over to the third base side of the pitcher's mound, so when the ball is bunted, you will be right on top of the play to catch the runner coming into third.

You also will be in position to see a play at second base in case the play is made that way. It will be tough if the bunt is slow and the play is made to first base. You will be away on the third base side of the field. You cannot help this, of course, and you have to call it from a distance just as you see it.

Watch carefully to see that every runner touches every base. If he knows you are watching him, he will be careful to touch every bag and will be afraid to try to skip one of them. If he knows you are watching him, he will have confidence in you and in all your decisions.

On plays around the bases try to get the right angle and keep your eyes glued to the fielder. Be sure he touches the runner with the ball in the gloved hand.

When a runner slides into home plate and the catcher tags the player with the glove, be sure the ball is held in the glove, or the runner will be safe.

When the batter hits a ball, follow it all the way with your gaze. The ball is likely to start fair and then roll foul, or start foul and curve into fair territory.

Study the temperament of each ball player and learn to distinguish between a ball player who is protesting in the desire to win and the ball player who is looking for trouble.

If you think the player is kicking because he hates to lose, listen a few seconds. The best ball players in the game will protest, if they think you have made a mistake that hurts their chances of winning, and they do it with no idea of causing trouble.

The other type of player kicks to impress the fans with his fighting spirit or to show up the umpire in a bad light. Get rid of this type quickly. Do not let them go far, for they will all but break up a ball game and get you in a jam.

Never associate with players off the field. If you meet them and they speak to you, return the greeting, but never refer to anything that happened in the game that day or at any time before. Never carry on long conversations with players on or off the field.

Never bear malice toward any player over what happens on the field, no matter how much trouble he caused you. Forget everything that happens in a game as soon as the game is over.

Watch your health. Take care of your throat and eyes. Use a good gargle on a doctor's prescription after each day's work. Use a good eye wash after every game. Dust collects in the eyes and may cause trouble.

Conduct yourself as a gentleman off the field and around your hotel. The dignity you display in public will add to the respect players and fans will show you on the field. The president of your league depends upon you to uphold the best traditions of your profession at all times.

My advice to young umpires is to use the old-fashioned rubber-inflated protector at first until you get some experience. The new fiber protector that is worn under the coat is likely to cause you some discomfort and interfere with your movements when you are new to the business. After you have been working for a few months, you can try out one of the light fiber protectors successfully.

The last thing you want to do is to worry over having had a bad day. When you honestly feel you have missed a strike or two, do not brood over it. If you have missed a couple of tag plays, do not let it get your goat. When you start doing that, you are on your way out and you might as well give up and go home. I have seen many an umpire fail because he worried himself sick over the few mistakes he made.

Young umpires are invited to ask me any questions they wish. Just send a self-addressed stamped envelope for the reply. I will gladly answer them.

Grandstand Umpiring

WHY FANS CANNOT SEE PLAYS WELL ENOUGH TO CHALLENGE UMPIRES' DECISIONS—INSIDE DOPE ON BALLS AND STRIKES—A CASE IN POINT

BASEBALL fans always have thought and always will think they can sit in the bleachers or the grandstand and call close plays better than an umpire can. We umpires take this as a sign that they are interested in the game and loyal to the home team and let it go at that.

If fans did not care how we called plays, they would not spend their money to come to the ball park, and the game of baseball would collapse.

Let us talk about it for a little while and see just how ridiculous it is to suppose that a man sitting in the grandstand can see a play better than an umpire. No matter where you sit, even if it is opposite first or third on the base lines, or back of the screen, the umpire is closer to the play than you are. The farther you are away from the play, the more deceiving are the angles that interfere with correct vision. Umpires know that they have to be right on top of a play to call it correctly, and even then they may make a mistake.

In the matters of balls and strikes, fans can sit 100 yards or more away in the bleachers and beat any umpire calling them. They do not realize that it is tough even when standing in the proper position right behind the catcher to judge the position of a hard-thrown ball when it crosses the area above the plate.

Batters stand in many different positions. Some have a crouch and others stand erect. Only the man in blue behind the catcher can judge whether the ball is too high or too low.

In making first base decisions, for instance, you must watch the foot of the runner as it touches the bag and listen for the ball to hit the first baseman's glove. An umpire, therefore, must not only have good eyes but good ears. Most fans watch the ball at a game and cannot hope to tell whether the ball hit the glove first or the runner's foot hit the bag first.

After all these years I have found that if an umpire calls the home ball player out on a close decision at first, fans immediately start yelling and booing; but if he calls a visiting player out on the same sort of play, he is cheered as a great umpire. Umpires know that with fans the heart is quicker than the eye.

Close decisions at other bases are even harder for

fans to judge from where they sit. Take a play at second where the catcher is trying to catch a man stealing. The second baseman gets the throw okay in his gloved hand, and puts the ball right down in front of the bag where the runner runs into it. Fans cannot see any tag made and think the runner got there, so they never believe this decision when it is made.

Again at second base on the same play the runner may make a hook slide around the bag and actually get there before the fielder puts the ball on him, or he may drop suddenly and make the fielder miss him entirely. This play cannot be seen from the stands usually on account of the angle from which the fans view it.

Umpires must learn to take a lot from the fans. Often when players rush toward an umpire and abuse him for a decision they do not like, fans say: "I would not be an umpire for anything, having to take all that abuse from players."

Then before fans have gotten through feeling sorry for the umpire, he makes a close decision that is against the home team. Sympathy is forgotten, and fans begin calling the umpire names and reaching for their pop bottles. Fans go to a game to see the home team win. Anything that hurts the home team, especially an umpire's decision, makes them mad.

Fans are getting better these days. We do not have nearly as many pop bottle showers as we used to have. This may mean that more women are coming to the games than ever before, and this naturally makes the crowd behave better.

Still in many leagues the old baseball atmosphere persists and fans continue to call 'em from the bleachers and throw bottles. If they would stop to think that the umpire must make 275 or more decisions in every game, that he is closer to the play than they are and at a better angle, that he is absolutely fair and square and calls 'em as he sees 'em, they would not go to extremes in their denunciation and their violence.

The men in blue are on the spot. They have to decide in a split second and cannot call every close one in favor of the home team because the plays just do not happen that way.

Fans should stop and think that their own opinion may be influenced not only by loyalty to the home team, but by a pool or a bet on the game.

Gambling is the greatest menace to the game of baseball, especially these pools for which tickets are sold. They not only lead to violence on the field, but with tampering with ball players or attempting to tamper with them. I do not beieve that any ball players have listened to outside influence in many years, and I know umpires have not. Umpires have not even been approached.

If an umpire is incompetent, he cannot last in the game. As long as he is out there to administer the rules of the game, let him be respected.

Following another set of umpires into a town sometimes leaves you wide open to attacks from fans for what the previous umpires have done. This is especially true since few fans know one umpire from another.

Umpires Kerin and Gifford were working a game in Nashville and when bleacher fans got on Kerin, he went over and challenged any one of them to come around to the dressing room after the game and have it out.

That did not help things at all and bottles began to fly, but the umpires got away safely after the game.

We came in the next day and the bleachers opened up on me right off by yelling:

"Kerin, you had better get the cops to look after you when this game is over, because we are after you and mean business."

They did not discover until midway the game that I was not Kerin.

And still they try to call close plays from where they sit!

Do Fans Like It?

An Umpire Gives His Views on Night Baseball —Points Out Differences from Player Angle—Baseball Then and Now

WHETHER baseball fans like night games or not is a question the fans themselves have answered. They like night baseball because they turn out for the after-supper games in greater numbers every season, especially if they happen to have a winning club in that city.

Judging from attendance records at night games in the Southern League, I would say that night baseball will be played more and more. They have tried it in the majors, with Cincinnati leading the procession, and it may be more widely introduced under the big tent as time goes on.

Night baseball draws crowds because many whose work will not allow them to attend during the day can attend at night. Not everybody has the convenient hours of an umpire or a ball player.

Night baseball has brought in a new group of people. Many of them have not been able to see a ball game, except now and then on Sunday, for many years.

I also think that a greater number of women attend night games than ever came to daytime games, because their homework is over and it gives them a chance to go out with their husbands. From where I stand on the ball field, I am in a position to judge whether a crowd is enjoying the game or not, and I think they get as much kick out of night baseball as they ever do in the day.

Little Rock, Nashville, and Atlanta had night baseball in the Southern in 1935. The Little Rock club played every night except Sunday. Two night games a week were played in Nashville and Atlanta. Night baseball kept those clubs in the league, and helped Atlanta set an all-time attendance record in 1935. One of the night games in Atlanta drew 19,266 paid admissions.

Umpiring problems are harder at night. It is very hard to judge balls and strikes, and trapped balls in the outfield are hard to see. Plays on the bases are harder to see than in the daytime. Ball players have a harder time seeing the ball, especially certain types of pitching. Much of this can be helped if lighting systems would be improved.

Baseball games are played much the same at night as in the daytime. There are just as many close games and extra inning games.

Fast-ball pitchers with good control are the most

feared by batters at night. They cannot follow the break of the ball under the lights as well as they can in the daytime. A slow curve ball pitcher has no advantage at all at night, but a fast-breaking curve ball pitcher can get by fine.

Old-fashioned fans who grew up with the game do not like night baseball and never will, but most clubs are playing a greater proportion of their games in the afternoons, and that ought to take care of the old-timers.

If fans want night baseball, as they have shown they have, let us give it to them, even if it does make things harder on players and umpires.

* * *

Times have changed in baseball and in the life of an umpire in the 25 years that I have been wearing the blue.

When I first broke into the game, the players were rough and the crowds were rougher. Fights were frequent on the field among players. They did not hesitate to spike each other in sliding into bases. The language they used would make a wooden Indian blush.

Players rode to the park in buses, and often the people threw rocks at the visiting team after a game.

There were no dressing rooms for umpires. We usually had to dress in the tool house or behind a corner of the grandstand. The stands were usually built of wood and inadequate to hold big crowds.

However, the police were alert. They were at the park to maintain order, and at the first sign of trouble they came rushing out to the plate to protect players or umpires, and keep the crowd from lynching them.

Now baseball is a big industry. The grandstands are of steel and concrete with every convenience for players and umpires. The players are often college men who have learned to take orders from a coach and have learned not to kick on umpire's decisions. There is a spirit of sportsmanship coming into the game.

The crowds are better behaved too. They do not attempt to mob us umpires as often. I had just one bottle shower in 1935. That was in Memphis. I had only two in 1934, in Chattanooga and New Orleans. I used to have that many every week in the old days.

The police, however, have gone into a slump. There are three times as many at the park every day, but they are watching the game. They do not come on the run when trouble is starting. When we need one, we have to look all over the grandstand for them. They are just out for a pleasant afternoon.

That all means that human nature is getting better, that is, all but the policemen.

"Steamboat's" Speech

Text of Address at Baseball Meeting Defends the Profession and Urges Co-operation of Club Owners and Ball Players

THIS is an address I delivered before a meeting of the National Association of Professional Baseball Leagues in Louisville, Ky., on the subject "The Umpire, His Power and Authority."

A copy of this talk was requested by Commissioner K. M. Landis, and now is on file in his office:

Umpiring, in my judgment, is the most important and far-reaching of any one factor that enters into the successful conduct of professional baseball. It is by far the most exacting position on the diamond to fill to the satisfaction of the manager, the player, the public and the regularly constituted baseball authorities. The umpire, clothed as he is with unlimited and autocratic power under the playing rules, must exercise the utmost discretion and judgment in the application of that power. He must be a man of good physique, strong mind, clear eyes, even temperament, quick judgment and forceful enough in character to command the respect and acquiescence of all concerned in his rulings and decisions. He must so conduct himself at all times as to inspire confidence in his honesty and ability, and be able to impart to all observers his evident desire and intention to treat everybody with the utmost consideration and impartiality.

Baseball today would contain a great many more stars, if the playing side kept pace with the umpiring. Public opinion is too apt to pass judgment upon the arbiter. I do not hesitate to say that not one player out of five would stand half the abuse the most competent and ablest officials of the game are subjected to, and still be able to hold up his head, and continue on with the profession. Did it ever occur to you, if the fans got after the ordinary player as the players themselves get after the umpire, how many of our present stars of today would be driven back into business?

During the progress of a game, the umpire must be in absolute control of the situation at all times, yet he must be prepared to take considerable amount of abuse from the players, if it happens to be a closely-contested game.

He soons learns to distinguish between the spontaneous outburst of the player whose whole heart is in the play, and who, in the heat of excitement indulges in some protest and profanity as the result of a close decision. This sort of a fellow is always honest and earnest in his protest, and, for the moment believes he is right. As soon as his anger subsides he again becomes the earnest, sincere and gentlemanly player. This is the class of player who carries the fighting spirit so much to be desired on every ball club, but never gets into any serious trouble and does not have to be fined or removed from the game.

The bane of the umpire's existence is the grouch and the "sure-thing" manager or player who is always looking for the best of it in every decision that comes up. He is never satisfied, never out, never fooled at bat, never hits a foul ball if the ball is within three feet of the line either way, never runs out of line, never fails to touch the bag when running bases, never fails to put the ball on the runner and who never fails to inject himself into every dispute that arises during the program of play.

When this class of individual begins to cuss out the umpire, he does it in a manner so vicious and so vehement as to make his immediate removal an absolute necessity. If this particular offender happens to be a player of ability, his loss from the line-up during the balance of the game is a real handicap to his club and immediately calls down upon the head of the umpire the wrath and ill will of the spectators. Such players and managers are the real menace to the popularity, perpetuity and future success of baseball.

I do not believe in a quiet ball game, but absolutely no question of judgment should be ever taken against the umpire, unless the interpretation of the rules is wrong. A great many times a player's or manager's kicking develops a fight and later on into rowdyism. Everyone of us knows that certainly has no part in the national pastime.

One of the worst conditions that exists in a great many leagues is the panning the umpire receives from the newspapers and the write-ups the president gets which the fans read. They come out the next day and start on the umpire and league president and keep it up during the umpire's assignment in that town. As a matter of fact, the sporting editor writes part of his story from information he gets from the manager or player, and if it happened that a player or manager was chased from the game, the editor gets their side of it. I can say without fear that a great many of the writers exaggerate details of the game and criticize the work of the umpire. I can say from actual experience that every umpire is so taken up with his work that he forgets what teams are playing and what the inning is and in most times is surprised to find that the game is really over.

Did you ever realize that the umpire is always

pointed out on the street, and that he must use excellent diplomacy in every respect not to get into any arguments that would discredit the league, and to uphold the dignity and honor he must have, when he gets out on that diamond? I want to say that the quicker the umpire is given full protection, the quicker new men will be to enter the profession, and stick to it. I claim and it is a positive fact that there is not one umpire but who is tickled when he feels that he is umpiring a good game. I have never known any umpire who was not always trying to do his very best every moment that he was working, yet the riding and ragging from ball players and managers and the abuse he receives from the spectators from the action of ball players certainly will not help him in any way.

Let club owners see that all the police officers detailed to the game are distributed around through the bleachers and grandstand. I know of several parks where the police officers stick in one place, and never move during the game. When something does come up, they will all rise and stand in one spot trying to locate where the trouble started. They very seldom stop the bottle throwers.

Club owners must see that the umpire is absolutely protected at all times for the good of baseball.

Permit me to try to tell you of the conduct of the

majority of umpires off the ball field. I do not know of one that does not try to be a gentleman and who always avoid arguments when he is on the streets and in his hotel. Many times they take insults from fans and come near fighting, but they use good judgment so as to not lose the dignity and respect they expect to receive when they are on the ball field.

While the double system umpiring is the most effective and satisfactory and should be adopted in all leagues that can afford it, I am mindful of the fact that the smaller leagues cannot hope to follow this. Furthermore, the game needs new umpires just as it needs players. In Class D leagues, new men should be breaking in constantly. They should be willing to start at reasonable salaries until they become accustomed to the work and have proven their ability. They should be advanced in the profession just as rapidly and easily as the player.

Too many club owners and especially in the smaller leagues, make a serious mistake of joining in with the crowd during the game and after the game in razzing the umpire, or in meeting him when he is coming to his dressing room and speaking to him harshly about his work.

I know from experience how helpful and encouraging it is to a young umpire to receive words of commendation and approval from club officials and managers. I want to say again it is exceptionally hard to secure the presence of honest, intelligent, unprejudiced, quick-witted, courageous umpires. The combination of attributes required is very difficult to find in any individual, and it is not easy to put one's hand upon a man who possesses any two of these several qualifications. Yet the efficient umpire must have them all.

The umpire must be intelligent. By intelligence I do not mean that he must have education or culture. The best umpire in the world might not shine as a scholar in a gathering of college professors, but he could outclass the entire faculty of any university in America in promptly and quickly deciding the fine points of a game of baseball. That is because he has the peculiar quality of intelligence required for his duties.

An umpire must be honest. A crooked umpire at a ball game is as offensive as a scoundrelly jurist on the bench. His power to harm the sport is even greater than that of a judge to bring law into reproach. The umpire does not deal with legal technicalities, whose veiled meaning needs to be explained by citations of other judges in other cases in other courts. He must hand down his decisions instantly before an audience of hundreds who know baseball law as well as he, or think they do.

So in behalf of the sport we love, to the exploitation of which the umpire is absolutely essential; because as Americans we are committed to fair play, I bespeak for the baseball umpire the same consideration that we extend the wearer of the ermine on the bench. I am happy to tell you that there is no single instance on record in the history of the game when an umpire has been charged with and proven guilty of any serious charge of dishonesty. I trust my words have left you with a thought that will help lighten the life of the baseball umpire.

Just Talking Shop

HOW THE SOUTHERN LEAGUE BASEBALL IS MADE—PRECAUTIONS TAKEN TO PRODUCE UNIFORM PRODUCT—THE BALL PLAYERS' ASSOCIATION

FEW fans realize what a great deal of mechanical equipment, carefully selected materials, and human skill go into the making of the Goldsmith baseball used in the Southern League. The company has made 4,500,000 baseballs in its time of operation, and every effort is made to turn out a uniform product.

Two sorts of centers, or cores, are used: the cork center and the rubber center, to meet the requirements of different leagues. The yarn that is wound around the cores is chemically tested for purity in wool and tensile strength. The best quality French horsehide is used for the covers. French horsehide has found to be smoother, more uniform in texture, and freer from blemishes than domestic hides.

The cores, which are made of uniform size, weight, and resiliency, are wound with yarn on machines the tension of which can be regulated and controlled at all times.

The liveliness of a baseball really is determined by the tension at which the yarn is wound rather than by the material used in the core. A tightly wound ball is livelier than a loosely wound ball.

Before the winding process starts, a double coating of cement is applied to the core to keep the yarn from slipping and another coating of cement on the uncovered ball to hold the cover fast.

The covers are cut from the finished hides by special dies that require an expert operator who knows his horsehides. The cutter must be able to judge the texture of each hide and cut his cover accordingly to allow for stretching. This assures that the baseball always will remain firm and that the cover cannot be loosened by batting. Very few men are qualified by experience and natural skill to operate a cover-cutting machine.

The covers, after they have been cut, are moistened thoroughly. Then they are given an undercoating of cement and applied to the wound cores. They are tacked in position and the hand-sewing operation begins. Workmen who sew baseballs are skilled through years of service and work fast and accurately. The thread used is the finest waxed linen thread tested for weight and strength.

After the covers have been stitched on, the balls are dried. This contracts the cover, fixes the cement, and results in a firm ball of even texture the cover of which will not slip nor loosen. The balls then are stamped, weighed and measured, and packed for sale.

Every operation in the making of a baseball is checked and rechecked by instruments for weight, size, texture, resiliency, and firmness as the manufacturing process goes along. All defective baseballs are thrown out or sold as cheaper grades of unofficial baseballs.

The company that makes the baseballs for the Southern League has been manufacturing them ever since the old National was a 12-club circuit. It has functioned through the stormy days of warfare between the Federal and the American Leagues. Ball players have come and gone and managers have become famous and dropped out of the picture, but the integrity of the manufacturer and the quality of his product has stood up. Many of the machines used in winding and cutting processes have been developed at this plant, and much has been contributed thereby to keeping the game up to standard.

EVERY baseball player and umpire should be a member of the Association of Professional Ball Players of America. It is an organization financed and maintained by baseball men for the relief of sickness and want among the members of the profession. The outstanding public function promoted on behalf of the organization is the annual all-star baseball game between teams picked from the two major leagues.

The names of the 1935 officers are a guide to the high caliber of the association:

George Stovall, President.
Charles Deal, First Vice President.
Andy High, Second Vice President.
Art Kruger, Third Vice President.
Charles Chech, Treasurer.
Russ Hall, Secretary.
Charles Grimm, Walter Maranville, Nick Altrock, Eddie Collins, Wade Killifer, Art Griggs, John J. Evers, Bert Niehoff, Truck Hannah, Mickey Cochrane—Directors.
Judge Emil Fuchs, Clark Griffith—Advisory Counsel.

The membership is composed of ball players, umpires, managers, scouts, fans and coaches, both active and inactive. There are many honorary members who are given a life membership for a fee of $5. Such members, however, pay no annual dues nor receive any benefits. Yearly dues for members from the major Leagues are $10; Class AA, $7.50; Classes A, B, C, and D, $5; retired players, $5.

The association has had a most successful career.

It has paid out in benefits to its members over $118,-000 since it was founded in 1933. A total of 234 cases have been cared for in every state in the Union and in several foreign countries. One hundred and ten of these cases were death cases. A monthly report of all activities and a financial report are mailed to the office of Commissioner K. M. Landis. The membership elects all officers.

The association does not render assistance to able-bodied men who do not care to work, nor does it carry any accident benefits, nor a pension system. Each case is treated separately on its merits and assistance given as required.

The association has 1,700 members and is a wholesome influence in the game of baseball.

The Big Parade

STARS OF SOUTHERN LEAGUE WHO WENT UP IN "STEAMBOAT'S" TIME—DIXIE SERIES EXPERIENCES —A PLAYER MOBBED BY FORT WORTH FANS

A LOT of ball players have passed across my path since 1919 when I came into the Southern League as umpire, and many of them were youngsters who graduated into the majors. Changes come fast in baseball and they either go up or down rapidly. Here are the names of some I have seen go on to faster company:

Luke Appling, shortstop, Atlanta 1930, to White Sox.

Bruce Campbell, outfielder, Little Rock 1930, to White Sox.

Louis Chiozza, third baseman, Memphis 1933, to Phillies.

Hazen Cuyler, outfielder, Nashville 1923, to Pirates.

Linus Frey, shortstop, Nashville 1934, to Brooklyn.

Earl Grace, catcher, Little Rock 1928, to White Sox.

James Dykes, third baseman, Atlanta 1919, to Athletics.

Charles Grimm, first baseman, Little Rock 1919, to Pirates.

George Haas, outfielder, Atlanta 1926, to Athletics.

Arnel Hale, third baseman, New Orleans 1931, to Cleveland.

Travis Jackson, shortstop, Little Rock 1922, to Giants.

Harold Lee, outfielder, Atlanta 1929, to Brooklyn.

Bud Clancy, first baseman, Little Rock 1926, to White Sox.

Samuel Leslie, first baseman, Memphis 1929, to Giants.

Alphonse Lopez, catcher, Atlanta 1929, to Brooklyn.

Buddy Myers, third baseman, New Orleans 1925, to Senators.

Andy Reese, outfielder, Memphis 1926, to Giants.

Howard Lisenbee, pitcher, Memphis, to Washington.

Dan Taylor, outfielder, Memphis 1927, to Cubs.

Cecil Travis, third baseman, Chattanooga 1933, to Washington.

Pie Traynor, third baseman, Birmingham, to Pirates.

Sam West, outfielder, Birmingham 1926, to Washington.

Dibrell Williams, shortstop, Little Rock 1929, to Athletics.

Paul Andrews, pitcher, Mobile 1929, to Yankees.

Larry Benton, pitcher, Memphis 1922, to Boston Nationals.

Clinton Brown, pitcher, New Orleans 1929, to Cleveland.

Lloyd Brown, pitcher, Memphis 1927, to Washington.

Lance Richbourg, outfielder, Nashville 1926, to Washington.

Phil Collins, pitcher, New Orleans, to Phillies.

Alvin Crowder, pitcher, Birmingham 1926, to Washington.

Benjamin Frey, pitcher, Nashville 1929, to Cincinnati.

Irving Hadley, pitcher, Birmingham 1926, to Washington.

Melvin Harder, pitcher, New Orleans 1929, to Cleveland.

Charles Lucas, pitcher, Nashville 1922, to Giants.

Fred Marberry, pitcher, Little Rock 1923, to Washington.

Louis Newsome, pitcher, Little Rock 1931, to Cubs.

George Pipgras, pitcher, Atlanta-Nashville 1925, to Yankees.

Robert Smith, pitcher, New Orleans 1922, to Boston Nationals.

Arthur (Dazzy) Vance, pitcher, New Orleans 1921, to Brooklyn.

Earl Whitehill, pitcher, Birmingham 1922, to Detroit.

Harley Boss, first baseman, Chattanooga 1932, to Cleveland.

Hank Deberry, catcher, New Orleans 1921, to Brooklyn.

Poco Taitt, outfielder, Nashville 1927, to Boston.

* * *

I have worked in seven Dixie Series play-offs between the pennant winners of the Southern and the Texas leagues. Southern League umpires working with me have been Bill Brennan, Buck Campbell and John Quinn. The series in which I worked (winners named first) were:

1924—Fort Worth vs. Memphis.
1927—Wichita Falls vs. New Orleans.
1929—Birmingham vs. Dallas.
1931—Birmingham vs. Houston.
1932—Chattanooga vs. Beaumont.
1933—New Orleans vs. San Antonio.
1934—New Orleans vs. Galveston.

Texas League fans are very fair.

The Texas League umpires with whom I worked—Ballafant, Kober, Coe, Hunter, Sears and Barr—were efficient and ideal men to work with.

We had little or no trouble in these Dixie Series games. One peculiar incident was the time that Texas fans turned on a ball player, instead of the umpire, and plain clothes men had to rescue him.

It was in 1924 when Memphis was playing in Fort Worth. I called Turner Barber of Memphis out on a close play. He began to show off and, after a minute or two, I ordered him out of the game. The fans were on my side for some reason and after the game they closed in on Barber. Plain clothes men had to surround him and draw their pistols to keep the crowd back.

It was in this same game that First Baseman Kraft, of Fort Worth, came to bat in the first inning and struck out. Manager Jakie Atz shouted so all could hear that the next time Kraft came up he would blast one over the fence. Sure enough, Kraft hit a homer the next two times he came to bat.

Jake Atz was one of the greatest managers in the minors. He nearly broke up the league and the Dixie Series by winning pennants with Fort Worth.

* * *

The Texas League has won 9 out of 15 Dixie Series that had been played through 1935. The Southern League had won five in a row from 1931 through 1934 when Bert Niehoff brought the series decision back to Texas with his Oklahoma City club.

Questions and Answers

KNOTTY PROBLEMS MET WITH SHORT ANSWERS—A FEW QUERIES FROM UMPIRE'S FAN MAIL—INCLUDES DEFINITION OF INFIELD FLY

HERE are some of the baseball problems that have been asked me recently and my answers may solve a knotty question about the rules for the reader:

Q. *If a batted ball hits home plate and bounds into fair territory, is it a fair or a foul ball?*

A. It is a fair ball if it settles on fair ground.

Q. *Can a batter step out of his box after he steps into it?*

A. Yes; but before pitcher pitches the ball and telling the umpire and asks the umpire to call time.

Q. *A batter hits a ball to an infielder who throws to first base; the first baseman juggles the ball and the runner crosses the bag before the first baseman holds the ball securely; is the runner safe or out?*

A. The runner is safe. The first baseman must hold the ball securely before the runner reaches the bag.

Q. *The pitcher has the ball in his glove but is not standing on the rubber. The pitcher makes a move to catch the runner off first base. Is this a balk?*

A. No balk. The pitcher can bluff a throw to first base as many times as he wants to as long as his foot is not on the rubber.

Q. *A fielder going after a batted ball runs into the umpire and the runner on first going to second reaches the bag safely; the fielder claims the umpire interfered with him and demands runner be sent back to first. What should the umpire do?*

A. This play stands as if the fielder had not run into the umpire.

Q. *Can a batter take a couple of pitches right handed and then change over to left handed?*

A. The batter may take two pitches as a right hander, then turn and take the next one left handed if he chooses to do so.

Q. *The runner standing on a bag is hit by a batted ball. Is he out?*

A. He is out. The rule makes no exception as to where the runner shall stand, it says he is out.

Q. *Batter, with two strikes already called on him, calls "Time" just as the pitcher delivers the ball. The ball comes over the plate and the umpire calls the batter out. Was this correct?*

A. Yes. The batter cannot ask for time after the pitcher has delivered the ball.

Q. *What is an infield fly?*

A. With none out or one out with first and second occupied or first, second and third occupied, a fly ball that can be handled by an infielder is an infield fly. The runners can advance at their peril.

Q. *After three balls have been called on the batter, the pitcher makes a balk with first and second occupied. Can the batter take his base?*

A. The runners advance one base, but the batter remains at the plate as no batter can be sent to first base on a balk.

Q. *A runner is on first; the batter hits a ground ball to the first baseman; the first baseman touches first then throws to second. Must the runner be tagged with the ball by the fielder at second, or can he merely touch the bag?*

A. The fielder must tag the runner coming into second.

Q. *When a batted ball hits the umpire on fair ground is the batter out?*

A. No. The batter is entitled to first base. If any runners are on base they must return to the last base they occupied, unless there are three on base. In this case, the man on third can score and the batter goes to first.

Q. *Can a coach, say at third base, touch the runner who has just hit the ball over the fence without the runner being called out?*

A. I would not call the runner out if he hit the ball clear out of the park, if the coacher touched him at third base.

Q. *What constitutes running out of line?*

A. That is a matter left to the judgment of the umpire. If the umpire believes the runner runs outside the three foot line, he calls the runner out; if not, safe.

Q. *The bases are filled, and two men are out, the batter hits to the third baseman, who throws to second base but the throw is too late and misses the runner, but the runner between second and third is trapped, and no one covering third base but later is tagged. The man on third in the meantime crosses home plate and was going to the dugout, when the out was made. Does the run count?*

A. No. The runner who was on second was forced to advance, and he was put out before reaching third base, why, it was a force out, and the run could not score.

Index